Trends in Lake Chemistry in Response to Atmospheric Deposition and Climate in Selected Class I Wilderness Areas in Colorado, Idaho, Utah, and Wyoming, 1993–2009

By M. Alisa Mast and George P. Ingersoll

Prepared in cooperation with the U.S. Department of Agriculture Forest Service, Air Resource Management

Scientific Investigations Report 2011–5123

U.S. Department of the Interior
U.S. Geological Survey

U.S. Department of the Interior
KEN SALAZAR, Secretary

U.S. Geological Survey
Marcia K. McNutt, Director

U.S. Geological Survey, Reston, Virginia: 2011

For more information on the USGS—the Federal source for science about the Earth, its natural and living resources, natural hazards, and the environment, visit http://www.usgs.gov or call 1-888-ASK-USGS

For an overview of USGS information products, including maps, imagery, and publications, visit http://www.usgs.gov/pubprod

To order this and other USGS information products, visit http://store.usgs.gov

Suggested citation:
Mast, M.A., and Ingersoll, G.P., 2011, Trends in lake chemistry in response to atmospheric deposition and climate in selected class I wilderness areas in Colorado, Idaho, Utah, and Wyoming, 1993–2009: U.S. Geological Survey Scientific Investigations Report 2011–5123, 44 p.

Contents

Figures

Tables

Conversion Factors

Inch to SI

Multiply	By	To obtain
	Length	
inch (in.)	2.54	centimeter (cm)
inch (in.)	25.4	millimeter (mm)
foot (ft)	0.3048	meter (m)
mile (mi)	1.609	kilometer (km)
	Area	
square mile (mi^2)	259.0	hectare (ha)
square mile (mi^2)	2.590	square kilometer (km^2)
	Volume	
ounce, fluid (fl. oz)	0.02957	liter (L)
gallon (gal)	3.785	liter (L)

Temperature in degrees Celsius (°C) may be converted to degrees Fahrenheit (°F) as follows:

°F=(1.8×°C)+32

Temperature in degrees Fahrenheit (°F) may be converted to degrees Celsius (°C) as follows:

°C=(°F-32)/1.8

Vertical coordinate information is referenced to the insert datum name (and abbreviation) here, for instance, "North American Vertical Datum of 1988 (NAVD 88)".

Horizontal coordinate information is referenced to the insert datum name (and abbreviation) here, for instance, "North American Datum of 1983 (NAD 83)".

Specific conductance is given in microsiemens per centimeter at 25 degrees Celsius (µS/cm at 25 °C).

Concentrations of chemical constituents in water are given in microequivalents per liter (µeq/L).

Elevation, as used in this report, refers to distance above the North American Vertical Datum of 1988.

Abbreviations

ANC	Acid neutralizing capacity
ARML	Air Resources Management Laboratory
CASTNET	Clean Air Status and Trends Network
Forest Service	United States Department of Agriculture Forest Service
HNO_3	Nitric acid
NADP	National Atmospheric Deposition Program
NEI	National Emission Inventory
NH_3	Ammonia
NO_x	Nitrogen oxide
NWIS	National Water Information Service
RKT	Regional Kendall test
RMSN	Rocky Mountain Snowpack Network
SKT	Seasonal Kendall test
SNOTEL	National Resources Conservation Service Snow Telemetry Network
SO_2	Sulfur dioxide
USEPA	United States Environmental Protection Agency
USGS	U.S. Geological Survey
WRAP	Western Regional Air Partnership

Trends in Lake Chemistry in Response to Atmospheric Deposition and Climate in Selected Class I Wilderness Areas in Colorado, Idaho, Utah, and Wyoming, 1993–2009

By M. Alisa Mast and George P. Ingersoll

Abstract

In 2010, the U.S. Geological Survey, in cooperation with the U.S. Department of Agriculture Forest Service, Air Resource Management, began a study to evaluate long-term trends in lake-water chemistry for 64 high-elevation lakes in selected Class I wilderness areas in Colorado, Idaho, Utah, and Wyoming during 1993 to 2009. The purpose of this report is to describe trends in the chemical composition of these high-elevation lakes. Trends in emissions, atmospheric deposition, and climate variables (air temperature and precipitation amount) are evaluated over a similar period of record to determine likely drivers of changing lake chemistry.

Sulfate concentrations in precipitation decreased over the past two decades at high-elevation monitoring stations in the Rocky Mountain region. The trend in deposition chemistry is consistent with regional declines in sulfur dioxide emissions resulting from installation of emission controls at large stationary sources. Trends in nitrogen deposition were not as widespread as those for sulfate. About one-half of monitoring stations showed increases in ammonium concentrations, but few showed significant changes in nitrate concentrations. Trends in nitrogen deposition appear to be inconsistent with available emission inventories, which indicate modest declines in nitrogen emissions in the Rocky Mountain region since the mid-1990s. This discrepancy may reflect uncertainties in emission inventories or changes in atmospheric transformations of nitrogen species that may be affecting deposition processes. Analysis of long-term climate records indicates that average annual mean air temperature minimums have increased from 0.57 to 0.75 °C per decade in mountain areas of the region with warming trends being more pronounced in Colorado. Trends in annual precipitation were not evident over the period 1990 to 2006, although wetter than average years during 1995 to 1997 and drier years during 2001 to 2004 caused a notable decline in precipitation in the middle part of the record.

Many significant trends were evident in lake-water concentrations in the study lakes. About 70 percent of lakes had significant trends in specific conductance, pH, calcium, and sulfate concentrations, whereas less than 20 percent had trends in chloride and nitrate concentrations. Despite widespread declines in sulfate deposition, decreases in lake-water sulfate concentrations were mostly limited to lakes in the Zirkel/Flat Tops Mountains. Because sulfate in these lakes is derived primarily from atmospheric sources, lake chemistry in these two areas appears to be responding to regional and local declines in sulfur dioxide emissions. Many lakes showed upward trends in sulfate concentrations as well as acid neutralizing capacity and calcium concentrations. Upward trends in dissolved constituents appeared to be partly explained by a decline in precipitation between 1995 and 2002, which may have increased base-flow contributions to some lakes. Air temperatures, which increased throughout the region, also may have been a factor in lake-water chemical trends. Warming in alpine areas might increase rates of mineral weathering or cause enhanced melting of ice features such as permafrost, rock glaciers, and glaciers. The effect of melting ice on the chemistry of the study lakes is difficult to assess due to the unknown extent of permafrost as well as a lack of detailed hydrologic data. The notable increases in sulfate concentrations may indicate that warming is enhancing the rate of pyrite weathering, perhaps related to availability of oxygen. Another potential effect of warming might be to increase the frequency of freeze-thaw cycles in alpine areas. This mechanism might provide a possible explanation for the increases in acid neutralizing capacity in addition to sulfate that was observed at many of the lakes.

Introduction

High-mountain environments are sensitive to changes in atmospheric pollution and climate and may provide early warning indicators for change in more resistant ecosystems of higher-order watersheds (Williams and Tonnessen, 2000). Despite their vulnerability to environmental disturbance, these ecosystems generally have been monitored to a lesser degree than other landscape types in the United States. The rapid growth of urban areas in the Rocky Mountain region has increased concern about the environmental effects of atmospheric contaminants on high-elevation ecosystems, particularly in protected areas such as Class I wilderness areas in National Forests and in National Parks (Baron and others,

2010; Burns, 2004). Class I areas are those wilderness areas larger than 5,000 acres that were in existence as of August 7, 1977. The Class I designation affords these areas special protection from human-caused degradation of air-quality related values by air pollution (Peterson and others, 1992). Nearly all sulfur dioxide (SO_2) emissions and more than 70 percent of nitrogen oxide (NO_x) emissions in the Rocky Mountain region is thought to be produced by fossil-fuel combustion in urban areas and by electric utilities (Peterson and others, 1998). SO_2 is of environmental concern because it can be oxidized in the atmosphere to sulfate, which not only causes visibility impairment but is a major component of acidic deposition (Peterson and others, 1998). Many high-elevation lakes and streams in the Rocky Mountain region are particularly sensitive to acidic deposition because they are underlain by bedrock types that have little capacity to buffer acidic inputs (Clow and others, 2002). In addition, most precipitation at high elevations accumulates in a seasonal snowpack, which serves as a reservoir for sulfate and other atmospheric contaminants that are released to surface water over a relatively short period during spring snowmelt (Campbell and others, 1995; Williams and others, 1996; Turk and Campbell, 1987).

Perhaps of more pressing concern in the Rocky Mountain region is the effect of atmospheric nitrogen deposition on alpine ecosystems (Williams and others, 1996; Baron and others, 2000). When nitrogen deposition exceeds uptake by plant and microbial communities, the system becomes nitrogen saturated, and nitrate is leached from soils into surface waters (Burns, 2004). Studies in Colorado indicate some high-elevation catchments in the Front Range are at an advanced stage of nitrogen saturation and that harmful effects on aquatic and terrestrial ecosystems are already occurring (Wolfe and others, 2003; Baron, 2006; Bowman and others, 2006).

During the past several decades, atmospheric pollution has declined throughout large regions of North America in response to reductions in anthropogenic emissions implemented by the Clean Air Act Amendments of 1990 (Stoddard and others, 2003). In eastern North America, improvements in precipitation chemistry and recovery of streams in response to these reductions have been documented by numerous studies (Driscoll and others, 2003; Kahl and others, 2004; Burns and others, 2006). In mountainous regions of the Western United States, the response of surface-water chemistry to changes in atmospheric deposition has been more difficult to evaluate because of a scarcity of long-term monitoring networks.

Alpine ecosystems also are facing potentially dramatic changes as a result of global warming given that increases in air temperatures and climate variability are expected to be most pronounced at northern latitudes and high elevations (Bradley and others, 2004). Even small temperature changes can have substantial hydrologic, chemical, and biological effects in alpine and subalpine environments where the depth and duration of snow cover is a major control of watershed processes (Koinig and others, 1998). Notable increases in

solute concentrations have been reported for numerous alpine lakes in Europe (Sommaruga-Wögrath and others, 1997; Tait and Thaler, 2000; Mosello and others, 2002; Rogora and others, 2003). These chemical changes have been attributed to enhanced weathering rates and increased biological activity caused by rising air temperatures (Sommaruga-Wögrath and others, 1997). More recent studies have indicated the effect of climate warming on increasing surface-water concentrations in alpine areas is related to enhanced melting of ice features such as permafrost, rock glaciers, and glaciers (Thies and others, 2007; Hill, 2008; Baron and others, 2009). In alpine lakes in Canada, climate shifts over the past decade were found to decrease nutrient concentrations and increase organic carbon, resulting in taxonomic shifts in the phytoplankton community (Parker and others, 2008). These studies illustrate that climate change may introduce a greater degree of variability in surface-water chemistry, which may mask trends resulting from improvements in atmospheric deposition of contaminants (Mosello and others, 2002).

Under the Clean Air Act of 1977 and its subsequent Amendments, Federal land management agencies are required to protect air-quality related values (AQRVs) in Class I Wilderness Areas. In addition, the 1964 Wilderness Act affords protection of all designated wilderness areas for both Class I and Class II air quality areas. AQRVs are sensitive resources that may be adversely affected by atmospheric deposition of acidic compounds (sulfur and nitrogen) and other toxic chemicals. In response to this mandate, the U.S. Department of Agriculture Forest Service (Forest Service) began identifying AQRVs in the National Forest System in the 1980s and implemented programs to inventory and monitor atmospheric deposition and sensitive receptors such as vegetation, soil chemistry, water chemistry, and aquatic life (Peterson and others, 1992). In Regions 2 and 4 of the Forest Service, water chemistry was identified as a key sensitive indicator and a program to monitor high-elevation lakes was implemented in the early 1990s. After nearly two decades of data collection, the USGS, in cooperation with the Forest Service Air Resource Management Program, conducted a comprehensive analysis of the long-term lake-chemistry data set collected in selected wilderness areas in Regions 2 and 4 of the Forest Service. A main objective of the study is to determine if changes in atmospheric deposition of contaminants in the Rocky Mountain region have resulted in measurable changes in the chemistry of high-elevation lakes. A second objective is to investigate linkages between lake chemistry and climate variability to improve understanding of the sensitivity of mountain lakes to climate change. Understanding how and why lake chemistry is changing over time in mountain areas is essential for effectively managing and protecting high-elevation aquatic ecosystems.

Purpose and Scope

The purpose of this report is to examine trends in the chemical composition of 64 high-elevation lakes in the Rocky Mountain region for the period 1993 to 2009. The lakes are located in 22 Class I wilderness areas on National Forest System lands throughout Colorado and parts of Idaho, Wyoming, and Utah. Trends in emissions, atmospheric deposition, and climate variables (air temperature and precipitation amount) are evaluated over a similar period of record.

Description of Study Lakes

The study lakes are located in selected Class I wilderness areas in Colorado and parts of Wyoming, Utah, and Idaho (table 1 and fig. 1). Most of the lakes are sampled as part of the Forest Service Air Resource Management program to protect aquatic ecosystems in Class I areas from the effects of air pollution (Berg and others, 2005). Lakes in three wilderness areas in Colorado (Flat Tops, Mount Zirkel, and Weminuche) are sampled as part of a USGS lake-monitoring program (Mast and others, 2011). The study lakes were selected because of their sensitivity to acidic deposition and their location relative to existing and proposed energy development and emission sources (Turk and Adams, 1983; Turk and Campbell, 1987; Berg and others, 2005). The lakes drain areas within the alpine and upper subalpine zones, and their watersheds are composed mainly of tundra, wet meadows, talus slopes, and bare rock (fig. 2). Scattered pockets of spruce and fir are present in the lower elevation watersheds. The lakes are oligotrophic and typically remain ice-covered for at least 6 months of the year (November to April). Hydrologic inputs to the lakes are dominated by snowmelt runoff and melting of permanent snowfields. Bedrock is variable across the study region, but most areas are underlain by slow-weathering silicate rock types such as granite and quartzite, which produces dilute surface water with low buffering capacity (Clow and others, 2002).

Data Sources and Methods of Analysis

This section describes sources of data presented in the report and statistical methods used to analyze temporal trends in these different data sets. Data characterizing the chemical composition of atmospheric deposition (wet and dry) were obtained from the National Atmospheric Deposition Program (NADP), the USGS Rocky Mountain Snowpack Network (RMSN), and the U.S. Environmental Protection Agency (USEPA) Clean Air Status and Trends Network (CASTNET). Climate data (air temperature and precipitation amount) were obtained from the National Resources Conservation Service Snow Telemetry (SNOTEL) network. Lake-chemistry data

were obtained from the Air Resource Management program in Forest Service Region 2 (Rocky Mountain) and Region 4 (Intermountain), and a USGS lake-monitoring program in Colorado.

The statistical methods used to test these data sets for temporal trends are suited for detecting long-term monotonic changes (generally increasing or decreasing over time) in constituent concentrations and climate variables. Temporal trends were analyzed for the period of record ranging from the early 1990s to the late 2000s. Although the start and end dates for the individual data sets varied by a few years, it was assumed that the records were sufficiently long that the overall trends would be comparable among data sets.

Precipitation Chemistry Data

Precipitation chemistry data from 23 primarily high-elevation (greater than 6,900 feet) NADP stations distributed throughout Colorado, Wyoming, Montana, and Utah (fig. 3) were analyzed for this study. NADP is a national network that collects weekly composite samples of wet-only precipitation that are analyzed for major dissolved constituents and nutrients at a central laboratory at the University of Illinois. Sample collection protocols, analytical methods, and quality-assurance procedures used by NADP are documented at *http://nadp.sws.uiuc.edu/*, accessed May 2011. Monthly precipitation-weighted mean concentrations and precipitation amount were retrieved from the NADP Web site. Mean concentrations provided by NADP are computed using only samples with complete and valid laboratory analyses and valid measurements of precipitation amount. Details of the sample screening process and computations can be found at *https://nadp.isws.illinois.edu/documentation/notes-AvMg.html*, accessed May 2011. Trends in monthly concentrations were calculated using the seasonal Kendall test (SKT), a non-parametric test that accommodates seasonality, outliers, missing data, and censored values (Helsel and Hirsch, 1992). Trends in concentrations were calculated for each NADP station using 12 seasonal groupings per year during the period 1988 through 2008 with the exception of the Wolf Creek Pass (CO91), Lost Trail Pass (MT97), and Brooklyn Lake (WY95) stations, which had slightly shorter periods of record (1991–2008 or 1993–2008). Trends in annual precipitation amount were computed by using the Mann Kendall test with Sen slope estimator (Helsel and Hirsch, 1992). Trends were not tested on hydrogen-ion concentrations determined from laboratory pH measurements because of contamination from the bucket lid that occurred prior to 1994 (*http://nadp.sws.uiuc.edu/documentation/advisory.html*, accessed May 2011). Hydrogen-ion concentrations determined from field pH measurements also had an incomplete record because field measurements were discontinued by NADP in 2004 (Lehmann and others, 2004). To extend the period of record, field hydrogen-ion concentrations from

Table 1. Characteristics of 64 study lakes in selected Class I wilderness areas in Colorado, Idaho, Utah, and Wyoming.

[Site no., site number from figure 1; USGS, U.S. Geolgical Survey; FS, U.S. Department of Agriculture Forest Service. Elevation above North American Vertical Datum of 1988]

Site no.	Lake name	State	Wilderness area	Mountain grouping	Latitude	Longitude	Collection agency	Elevation, in feet	Lake area, in square miles	Basin area, in square miles
1	Ingeborg Lake	Idaho	Sawtooth	Sawtooth Range	43.950	-115.0425	USGS	8,890	0.038	0.21
2	Harbor Lake	Idaho	Frank Church	Sawtooth Range	45.143	-114.5916	FS	8,927	0.029	0.25
3	No Name 4C1-048	Idaho	Sawtooth	Sawtooth Range	43.927	-114.9722	FS	9,055	0.026	0.12
4	Lake 502A	Idaho	Sawtooth	Sawtooth Range	44.027	-114.9675	FS	9,330	0.004	0.14
5	No Name 4C1-049	Idaho	Sawtooth	Sawtooth Range	43.914	-114.9691	FS	8,986	0.013	0.070
6	No Name 4C1-043	Idaho	Sawtooth	Sawtooth Range	44.031	-114.9589	FS	8,944	0.007	0.33
7	Florence Lake	Wyo.	Cloud Peak	Bighorn Mountains	44.348	-107.1806	FS	10,860	0.034	1.42
8	Emerald Lake	Wyo.	Cloud Peak	Bighorn Mountains	44.457	-107.3031	FS	10,249	0.054	1.12
9	Upper Frozen Lake	Wyo.	Bridger	Wind River Range	42.686	-109.1606	FS	11,440	0.036	0.12
10	Ross Lake	Wyo.	Fitzpatrick	Wind River Range	43.378	-109.6583	FS	9,682	0.761	17.3
11	Lower Saddlebag Lake	Wyo.	Popo Agie	Wind River Range	42.623	-108.9947	FS	11,263	0.052	0.69
12	Hobbs Lake	Wyo.	Bridger	Wind River Range	43.036	-109.6722	FS	10,066	0.027	1.45
13	Deep Lake	Wyo.	Bridger	Wind River Range	42.719	-109.1708	FS	10,509	0.092	0.80
14	Black Joe Lake	Wyo.	Bridger	Wind River Range	42.739	-109.1711	FS	10,259	0.123	3.88
15	Dean Lake	Utah	High Uintas	Uinta Mountains	40.679	-110.7608	FS	10,745	0.036	0.47
16	Walkup Lake	Utah	High Uintas	Uinta Mountains	40.811	-110.0385	FS	11,114	0.027	0.59
17	Fish Lake	Utah	High Uintas	Uinta Mountains	40.837	-110.0685	FS	10,685	0.059	0.81
18	Upper Ned Wilson Lake	Colo.	Flat Tops	Zirkel/Flat Tops	39.963	-107.3236	USGS	11,110	0.001	0.010
19	Lower NWL Packtrail Pothole	Colo.	Flat Tops	Zirkel/Flat Tops	39.968	-107.3233	USGS	11,085	0.002	0.051
20	Ned Wilson Lake	Colo.	Flat Tops	Zirkel/Flat Tops	39.962	-107.3236	USGS	11,100	0.003	0.21
21	Upper NWL Packtrail Pothole	Colo.	Flat Tops	Zirkel/Flat Tops	39.966	-107.3231	USGS	11,090	0.001	0.031
22	Seven Lakes	Colo.	Mount Zirkel	Zirkel/Flat Tops	40.896	-106.6808	USGS	10,733	0.015	0.080
23	Summit Lake	Colo.	Mount Zirkel	Zirkel/Flat Tops	40.546	-106.6803	USGS	10,316	0.007	0.038
24	Lake Elbert	Colo.	Mount Zirkel	Zirkel/Flat Tops	40.634	-106.7069	USGS	10,790	0.018	0.45
25	No Name 4E1-055	Colo.	Indian Peaks	Front Range	40.037	-105.6269	FS	11,227	0.034	0.86
26	Blue Lake	Colo.	Indian Peaks	Front Range	40.089	-105.6194	FS	11,306	0.036	1.02
27	Rawah Lake #4	Colo.	Rawah	Front Range	40.671	-105.9578	FS	11,473	0.038	0.36

Table 1. Characteristics of 64 study lakes in selected Class I wilderness areas in Colorado, Idaho, Utah, and Wyoming.—Continued

[Site no., site number from figure 1; USGS, U.S. Geolgical Survey; FS, U.S. Department of Agriculture Forest Service. Elevation above North American Vertical Datum of 1988]

Site no.	Lake name	State	Wilderness area	Mountain grouping	Latitude	Longitude	Collection agency	Elevation, in feet	Lake area, in square miles	Basin area, in square miles
28	King Lake	Colo.	Indian Peaks	Front Range	39.940	-105.6869	FS	11,437	0.016	0.077
29	Crater Lake	Colo.	Indian Peaks	Front Range	40.076	-105.6639	FS	10,305	0.039	1.07
30	Island Lake	Colo.	Rawah	Front Range	40.627	-105.9411	FS	11,129	0.024	0.20
31	Upper Middle Beartrack Lake	Colo.	Mount Evans	Front Range	39.571	-105.6067	FS	11,621	0.002	0.24
32	Upper Lake	Colo.	Indian Peaks	Front Range	40.156	-105.6811	FS	10,732	0.010	0.095
33	Frozen Lake	Colo.	Mount Evans	Front Range	39.578	-105.6583	FS	12,940	0.007	0.13
34	Abyss Lake	Colo.	Mount Evans	Front Range	39.586	-105.6592	FS	12,651	0.022	0.46
35	Kelly Lake	Colo.	Rawah	Front Range	40.626	-105.9594	FS	10,804	0.030	0.23
36	Deep Creek Lake	Colo.	Raggeds	Sawatch/Elk Mountains	39.008	-107.2397	FS	11,020	0.008	0.068
37	Blodgett Lake	Colo.	Holy Cross	Sawatch/Elk Mountains	39.408	-106.5364	FS	11,663	0.034	0.23
38	Moon Lake (Upper)	Colo.	Maroon Bells-Snowmass	Sawatch/Elk Mountains	39.164	-107.0594	FS	11,739	0.014	0.84
39	Booth Lake	Colo.	Eagles Nest	Sawatch/Elk Mountains	39.699	-106.3050	FS	11,460	0.014	0.22
40	South Golden Lake	Colo.	West Elk	Sawatch/Elk Mountains	38.778	-107.1828	FS	11,060	0.008	0.10
41	Upper Turquoise Lake	Colo.	Holy Cross	Sawatch/Elk Mountains	39.508	-106.5322	FS	11,299	0.011	0.50
42	Tabor Lake	Colo.	Collegiate Peaks	Sawatch/Elk Mountains	39.063	-106.6564	FS	12,290	0.008	0.081
43	Upper West Tennessee Lake	Colo.	Holy Cross	Sawatch/Elk Mountains	39.345	-106.4231	FS	12,041	0.004	0.39
44	Upper Willow Lake	Colo.	Eagles Nest	Sawatch/Elk Mountains	39.646	-106.1747	FS	11,381	0.010	0.48
45	Capitol Lake	Colo.	Maroon Bells-Snowmass	Sawatch/Elk Mountains	39.162	-107.0806	FS	11,581	0.033	0.56
46	Avalanche Lake	Colo.	Maroon Bells-Snowmass	Sawatch/Elk Mountains	39.143	-107.0981	FS	10,696	0.013	1.43

Table 1. Characteristics of 64 study lakes in selected Class I wilderness areas in Colorado, Idaho, Utah, and Wyoming.—Continued

[Site no., site number from figure 1; USGS, U.S. Geolgical Survey; FS, U.S. Department of Agriculture Forest Service. Elevation above North American Vertical Datum of 1988]

Site no.	Lake name	State	Wilderness area	Mountain grouping	Latitude	Longitude	Collection agency	Elevation, in feet	Lake area, in square miles	Basin area, in square miles
47	Brooklyn Lake	Colo.	Collegiate Peaks	Sawatch/Elk Mountains	39.049	−106.6564	FS	12,260	0.005	0.11
48	Upper Stout Lake	Colo.	Sangre De Cristo	Sangre de Cristo Range	38.350	−105.8908	FS	11,841	0.012	0.41
49	Lower Stout Lake	Colo.	Sangre De Cristo	Sangre de Cristo Range	38.353	−105.8892	FS	11,762	0.017	0.41
50	Upper Little Sand Creek Lake	Colo.	Sangre De Cristo	Sangre de Cristo Range	37.904	−105.5356	FS	12,379	0.003	0.10
51	Crater Lake, Sangre De Cristo	Colo.	Sangre De Cristo	Sangre de Cristo Range	37.576	−105.4950	FS	12,700	0.010	0.27
52	White Dome Lake	Colo.	Weminuche	Needle Mountains	37.709	−107.5525	USGS	12,540	0.008	0.15
53	Little Eldorado Lake	Colo.	Weminuche	Needle Mountains	37.713	−107.5458	USGS	12,507	0.004	0.18
54	Upper Grizzly Lake	Colo.	Weminuche	Needle Mountains	37.620	−107.5836	USGS	13,100	0.011	0.12
55	Upper Sunlight Lake	Colo.	Weminuche	Needle Mountains	37.628	−107.5797	USGS	12,545	0.023	0.31
56	Big Eldorado Lake	Colo.	Weminuche	Needle Mountains	37.713	−107.5433	USGS	12,504	0.022	0.43
57	Lower Sunlight Lake	Colo.	Weminuche	Needle Mountains	37.634	−107.5786	USGS	12,033	0.027	0.38
58	Lake south of Ute Lake	Colo.	Weminuche	San Juan/La Garita Mountains	37.636	−107.4428	FS	11,959	0.002	0.040
59	Lake south of Blue Lakes	Colo.	South San Juan	San Juan/La Garita Mountains	37.224	−106.6292	FS	11,860	0.004	0.050
60	Small Pond above Trout Lake	Colo.	Weminuche	San Juan/La Garita Mountains	37.652	−107.1564	FS	12,100	0.001	0.010
61	Middle Ute Lake	Colo.	Weminuche	San Juan/La Garita Mountains	37.648	−107.4741	FS	11,955	0.017	0.27
62	Glacier Lake	Colo.	South San Juan	San Juan/La Garita Mountains	37.258	−106.5864	FS	11,939	0.035	0.11
63	Lake above U-Shaped Lake	Colo.	La Garita	San Juan/La Garita Mountains	37.944	−106.8639	FS	12,900	0.003	0.12
64	U-Shaped Lake	Colo.	La Garita	San Juan/La Garita Mountains	37.942	−106.8606	FS	11,699	0.007	0.23

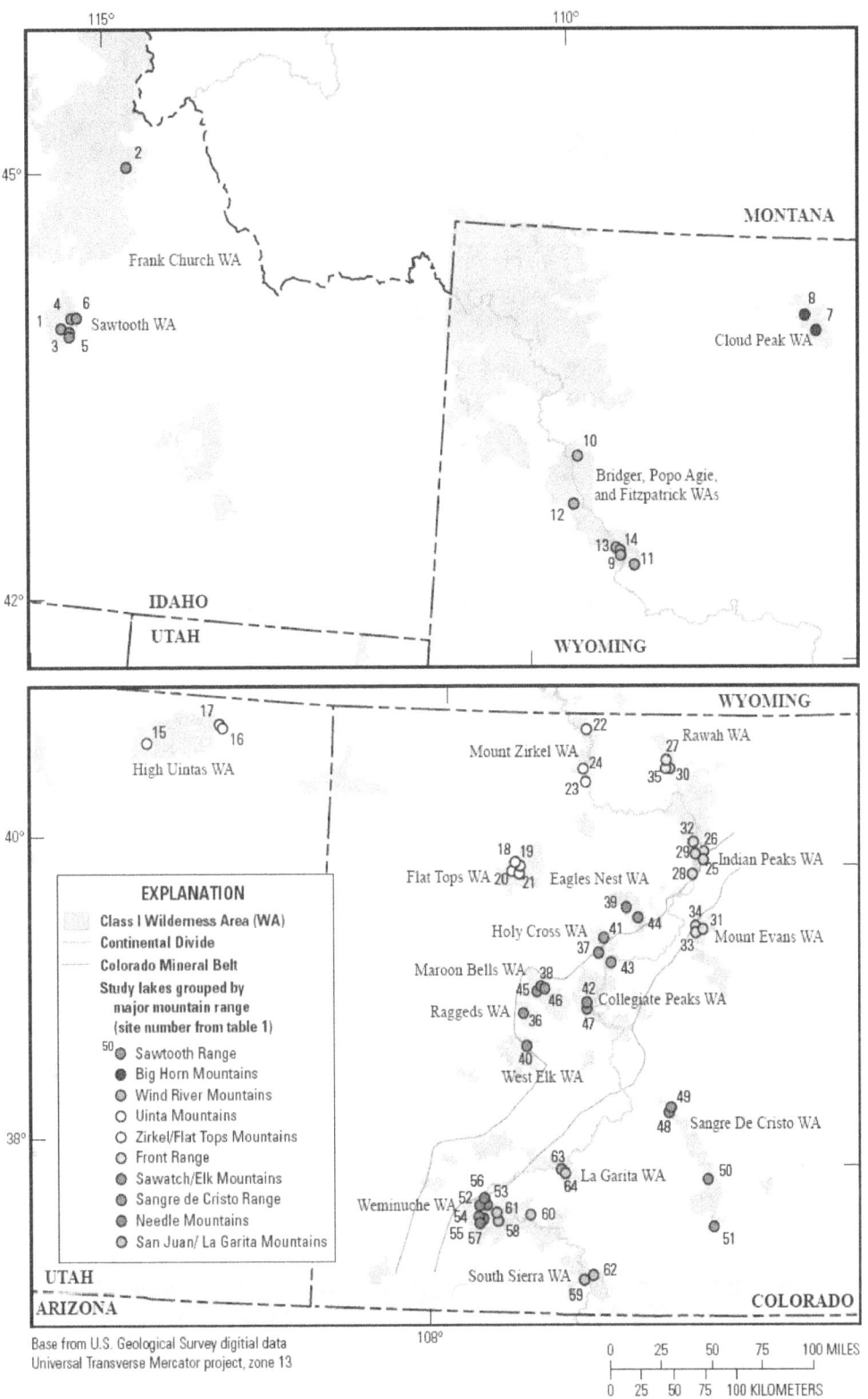

Figure 1. Class I wilderness areas in the Rocky Mountain region and study lakes grouped by major mountain range.

Figure 2. Photographs of (*A*) Brooklyn Lake in the Sawatch Mountains, (*B*) Lake Elbert in the Zirkel Mountains, (*C*) Upper Sunlight Lake in the Needle Mountains, and (*D*) Black Joe Lake in the Wind River Range.

2005 to 2008 were estimated based on simple linear regression relations developed between paired monthly laboratory and field hydrogen-ion concentrations for each station from 1994 to 2004. Values of r^2 for relations developed between laboratory and field hydrogen-ion concentrations ranged from 0.6 to 0.9. Trend results were considered highly significant if the p-value was less than 0.01 and moderately significant if the p-value was greater than 0.01 and less than or equal to 0.05.

Snowpack Chemistry Data

Snowpack-chemistry data were analyzed at 48 selected sites in the RMSN, which is a network of snow-sampling sites in the Rocky Mountain Region (fig. 3) that has been operated by the USGS since 1993 (*http://co.water.usgs.gov/projects/ RM_snowpack/*, accessed May 2011). Details of collection methods, analytical techniques, and quality-assurance procedures used by the RMSN are described in Ingersoll and others (2002). Briefly, depth-integrated snow samples are collected at each site in February, March, or April around the time of maximum snowpack accumulation to represent the majority

of annual snowfall in a single, composite sample. Samples are analyzed for pH, alkalinity, major dissolved constituents, and nutrients at the Colorado Water Science Center laboratory using approved analytical methods (Fishman and Friedman, 1989). Annual snowpack concentrations of ammonium, calcium, hydrogen, nitrate, and sulfate were retrieved for 48 sites for the period 1993 to 2008 from the RMSN Web site at *http:// co.water.usgs.gov/projects/RM_snowpack/*, accessed May 2011. All the RMSN sites had 16 years of data with the exception of Gypsum Creek, Old Faithful Fire Road, and Divide Peak, which had 15 years, and Loch Vale Forest, which had 14 years. Concentrations of ammonium, calcium, hydrogen, nitrate, and sulfate in winter wetfall at 17 selected NADP stations were used for comparison with snowpack chemistry. Winter concentrations were computed by volume-weighting monthly concentrations obtained from the NADP web site for November through April.

Statistical analyses comparing snowpack- and winter-wetfall chemistry were done at three geographic scales using one of two nonparametric tests: the Regional Kendall Test (RKT) or the SKT. The RKT is a modified version of the SKT that is used to test trends simultaneously at numerous

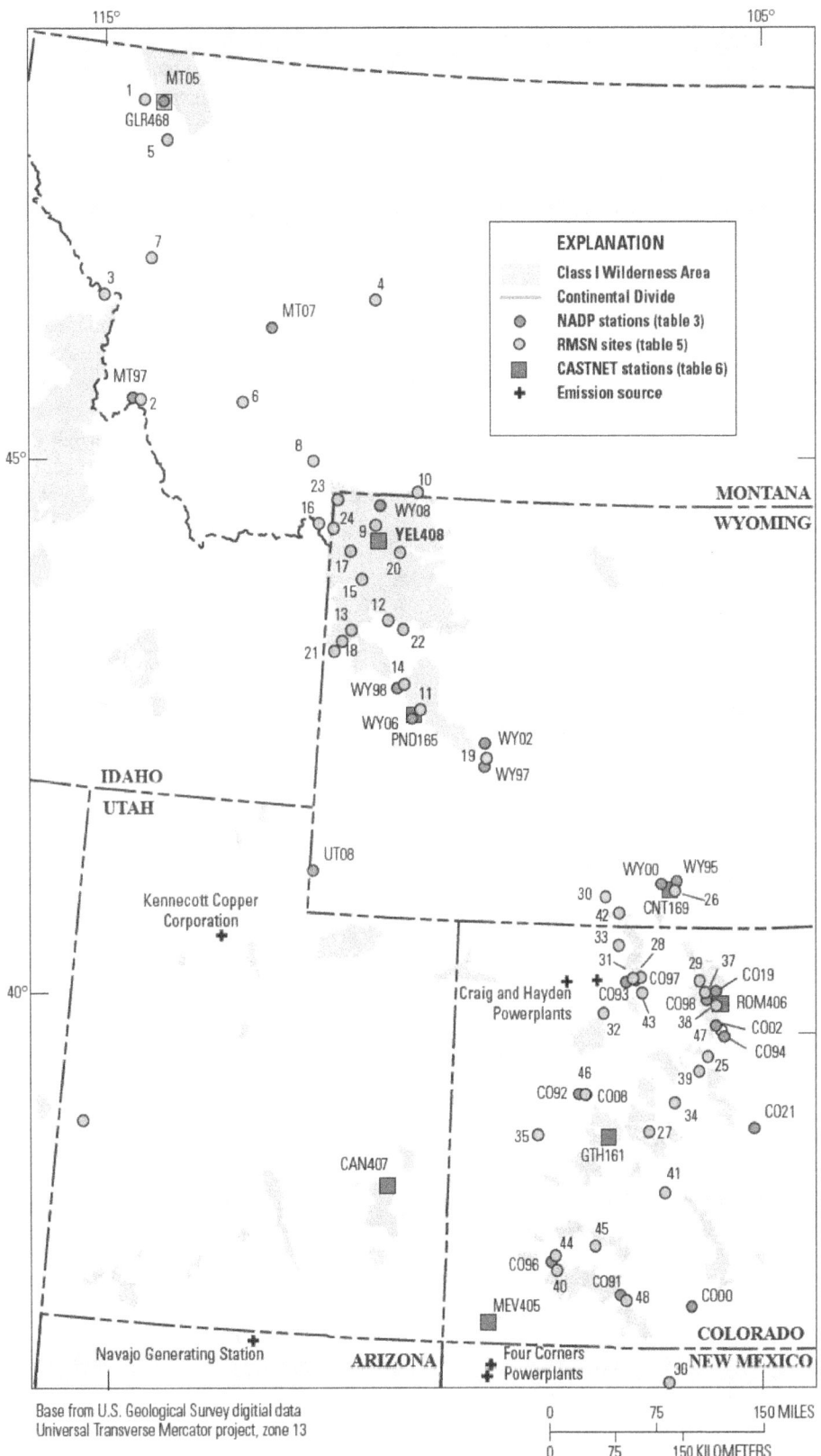

Figure 3. National Atmospheric Deposition Program (NADP) stations, Rocky Mountain Snowpack Network (RMSN) sites, and Clean Air and Status and Trends Network (CASTNET) stations in the Rocky Mountain region.

locations within a geographic region (Helsel and Frans, 2006; Helsel and others, 2006). First, the 48 snowpack sites and the 17 wetfall stations were tested as separate groups, using the RKT to test for regional trends representing the Rocky Mountain Region. Next, snowpack sites and wetfall stations were subdivided into three subregions (Northern Rockies, Central Rockies, and Southern Rockies) to examine subregional trends with the RKT. Finally, trend tests for individual sites were run using the SKT. Calcium concentrations at some of the snowpack sites were reported as less than the method reporting level of 3.1 microequivalents per liter (μeq/L). For these sites, the slope of the calcium trend was computed two ways, first by substituting 0.0 μeq/L for censored values and second by substituting 3.09 μeq/L. The final slope of the calcium trend is reported as the mean of two tests for sites with censored calcium concentrations.

Dry Deposition Data

Dry deposition data analyzed in this report were obtained from CASTNET (*http://www.epa.gov/castnet/*, accessed May 2011), which is the most extensive dry-deposition monitoring effort in the United States. The network measures weekly concentrations of sulfur and nitrogen compounds in gases and particulates and combines them with meteorological data to estimate dry-deposition rates. Data, collection methods, analytical techniques, and quality-assurance procedures are available at *http://www.epa.gov/castnet/*. Mean seasonal (Winter: Dec.–Feb., Spring: Mar.–May, Summer: June–Aug., Fall: Sept.–Nov.) concentrations of gaseous SO_2 and nitric acid (HNO_3) and particulate sulfate, nitrate, and ammonium were retrieved for eight stations from the CASTNET Web site (fig. 3). Trends in mean concentrations were tested with the SKT by using four seasons per year. Four sites were tested over the period 1990 to 2008; the remaining stations started later and were tested over the period 1995 to 2008.

Climate Data

Air temperature and precipitation amount were obtained from the National Resources Conservation Service SNOwpack TELemetry (SNOTEL) system, which is a network of automated snowpack and climate stations in mountain snowpack zones of the Western United States (*http://www.wcc.nrcs.usda.gov/snow/*, accessed May 2011). Data analyzed in this report were obtained for 144 SNOTEL stations in Colorado, Idaho, New Mexico, Utah, and Wyoming in and adjacent to the study-lake wilderness areas (fig. 4). Prepackaged data sets of daily minimum and maximum air temperature and monthly precipitation were retrieved from the National Resources Conservation Service Web site at *http://www.wcc.nrcs.usda.gov/climate/clim-data.html*, accessed May 2011. These data sets were quality assured by an automated probabilistic-spatial system that integrates climate mapping technology and climate statistics (Daly and others, 2004).

Even with the quality-assured data sets, some caution has been advised in application of SNOTEL air-temperature records for trend analysis due to changes in sensors and sensor placement over the period of operation (Julander and others, 2007). The most substantial bias appears to have been caused by replacement of the standard air temperature sensor with an extended range sensor starting in the mid-1990s. Readings from the extended range sensor are biased high by as much as 2 °C compared to the standard sensor with the greatest difference at the low end of the temperature range (Julander and others, 2007). To correct for this bias, the readings from the extended range sensor were corrected to a standard sensor reading by using a polynomial fit of the two sensor readings (fig. 5) at a station in Idaho (Mountain Meadows) where the sensors were run side by side for 18 months (Phil Morrisey, National Resources Conservation Service, unpub. data, 2010). Although this correction greatly improves the quality of the temperature records for trend analysis, it is possible that other artifacts related to site operation may exist in the data set. Annual mean and seasonal air temperature and precipitation amount at each station were computed from the corrected values and the stations were subdivided into 12 regional groupings based on major mountain ranges (fig. 4). Trends at individual stations were computed using the Mann-Kendall test and Sen slope estimator, and trends for each mountain group were computed using the RKT. To account for broad-scale climate patterns that might affect precipitation and temperature similarly for a group of stations, the results of the RKT test were corrected for spatial correlation using the method described in Sprague and Lorenz (2009).

Lake-Water Chemistry Data

Lake-chemistry data were obtained from two different monitoring programs, one operated by the USGS and the other operated by the Forest Service (table 1). The USGS has monitored lakes in three wilderness areas in Colorado (Flat Tops, Mount Zirkel, and Weminuche) as part of a long-term monitoring program (Mast and others, 2011). Lakes have been sampled 2 to 5 times per year during the open-water season (July–October) since the mid-1980s. Samples were collected from the shore close to the outlet or at the center of the lake from an inflatable boat. Because most of the study lakes are relatively small (less than 17 acres), the chemistry of the outlet and midlake samples should be similar (Clow and others, 2002). Samples were collected in polyethylene bottles and were field filtered within 24 hours of collection by using a peristaltic pump and a 0.45-μm membrane filter. Specific conductance and pH were analyzed in the laboratory on unfiltered sample aliquots, and acid neutralizing capacity (ANC) was determined by Gran titration (Gran, 1952). Chloride, nitrate, and sulfate concentrations were analyzed by ion chromatography on filtered, chilled sample aliquots; and calcium, magnesium, sodium, potassium, and silica concentrations were analyzed by inductively coupled plasma–atomic emission

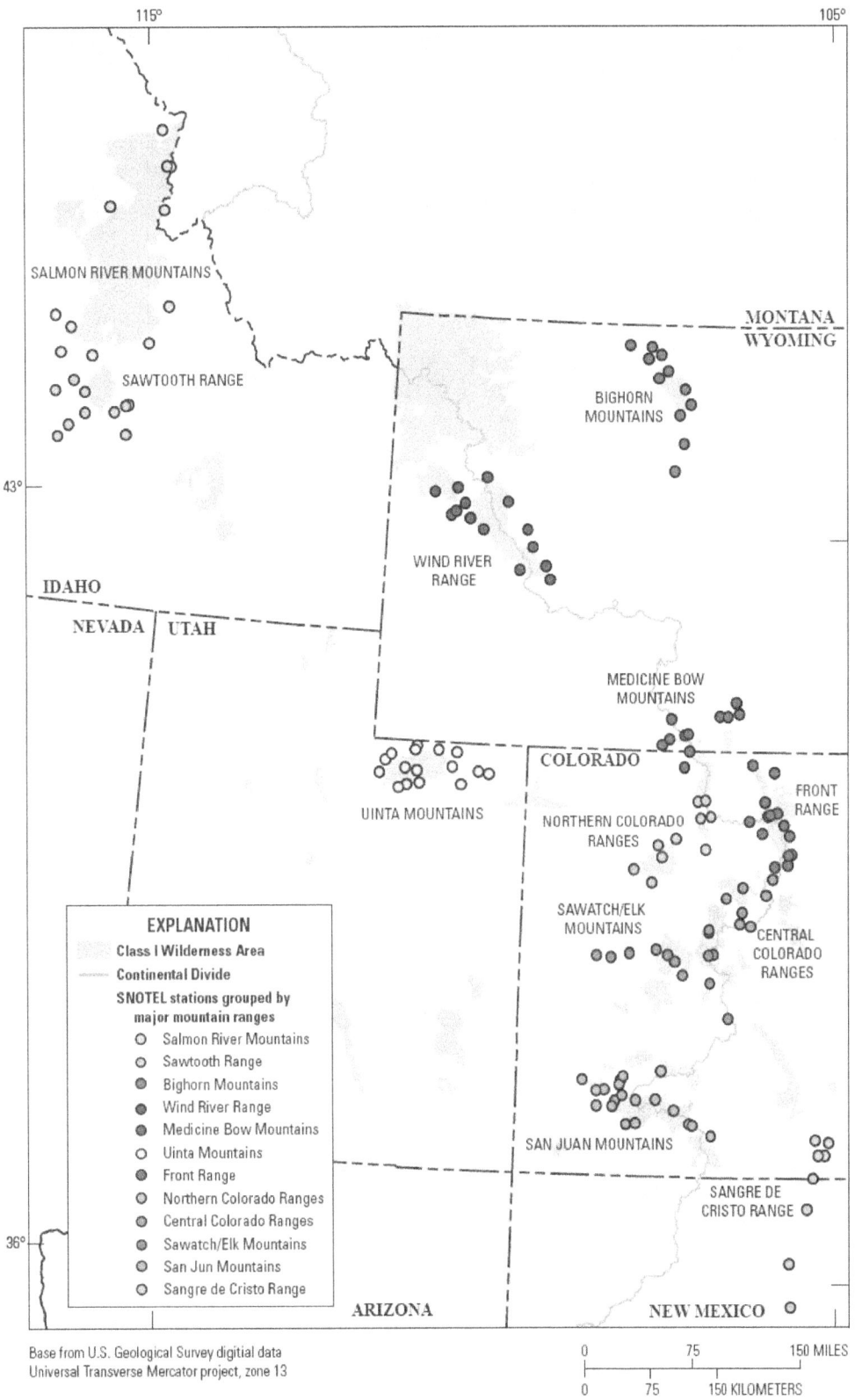

Figure 4. Snow Telemetry (SNOTEL) stations in Rocky Mountain region and geographic groupings used for trend analysis.

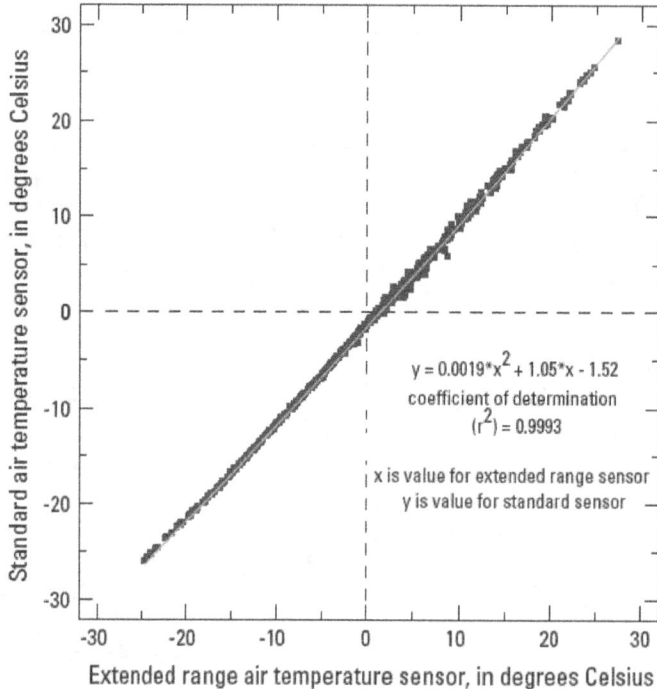

$$y = 0.0019 \cdot x^2 + 1.05 \cdot x - 1.52$$

coefficient of determination
$$(r^2) = 0.9993$$

x is value for extended range sensor
y is value for standard sensor

Figure 5.   Relation between daily air temperature measurements made with the extended range and standard sensors colocated at a Snow Telemetry (SNOTEL) station (Mountain Meadows) in Idaho.

spectroscopy on filtered, acidified aliquots. All chemical analyses were conducted at USGS laboratories using approved analytical methods (Fishman and Friedman, 1989) and results are stored in the USGS National Water Information System (NWIS) database available at *http://waterdata.usgs.gov/nwis* under the lake names listed in table 1.

The Forest Service monitors lakes in selected wilderness areas in the Rocky Mountain and Intermountain Regions as part of a directive under the Clean Air Act to protect Class I wilderness areas from the effects of air pollution (*http://www.fs.fed.us/air/*, accessed May 2011). Sampling at most lakes was initiated in the early 1990s, although a few lakes in the Wind River Range have been sampled since the mid-1980s. Grab samples were collected 1 to 3 times per year during the open-water season at the lake outlet or the center of the lake from an inflatable boat. Samples were collected in precleaned polyethylene bottles and stored in field coolers with ice packs during transport from the field site (Turk, 2001). Whole-water samples were shipped on ice as soon as possible to the Air Resources Management Laboratory (ARML), Fort Collins, Colorado, where they were vacuum filtered through a 0.45-μm membrane filter. ANC and pH were analyzed on the unfiltered sample aliquot using an automated titration system, and ANC was computed by the Gran titration method (Gran, 1952). Specific conductance was analyzed in the laboratory by a manual method before 2002 and an automated system afterwards. Chloride, sulfate, nitrate, fluoride, and phosphate concentrations were analyzed by ion chromatography.

Calcium, magnesium, sodium, and potassium concentrations were analyzed by atomic absorption spectroscopy until 1994 when ion chromatography was implemented. Analytical detection limits for methods used by ARML since 1994 are shown in table 2 and details on analytical methods can be found at *http://www.fs.fed.us/waterlab/*, accessed May 2011. All sample handling, analysis, storage, and data reporting conducted at ARML adhere to quality-assurance guidelines established in the Handbook of Methods for Acid Deposition Studies (U.S. Environmental Protection Agency, 1987). To monitor laboratory performance, the ARML has participated in an interlaboratory comparison conducted by the USGS since 1988 (*http://bqs.usgs.gov/srs/*, accessed May 2011). Results from the interlaboratory comparison indicate the quality of major-ion and nutrient data produced by ARML is comparable to USGS laboratories that analyzed lake samples collected by the USGS long-term monitoring program discussed previously.

To monitor quality control, the Forest Service lake-monitoring program has collected more than 160 field banks and 500 field replicates since sampling was initiated. A summary of the analytical results for the field blanks is provided in table 2. For most of the constituents, the 95th percentile concentrations for field blanks are less than three times the ARML detection limits, indicating bias introduced by contamination in the field and laboratory was minimal. The exceptions were calcium, sodium, and nitrate, which showed concentrations exceeding this level in as many as 16 percent of field blanks, perhaps indicating a low level of contamination

Table 2. Summary of concentration data for 167 field blanks collected as part of the U.S. Department of Agriculture Forest Service Air Resource Management lake-monitoring program, and analytical detection limits and range of concentrations in environmental samples provided for comparison.

[DL, detection limit; MRL, method reporting level is three times the DL; Percent exceedence is percentage of blank samples that had concentrations above 3xDL; ANC, acid neutralizing capacity, all concentrations in microequivalents per liter except specific conductance in microsiemens per centimeter at 25 Celsius; --, not applicable; <, less than]

Constituent or property	DL[1]	MRL	Field blanks		Environmental samples	
			95th percentile	Percent exceedence	10th percentile	90th percentile
Specific conductance	1.0	3.0	1.8	0	6.9	23.2
ANC by gran titration	--	--	7.8	--	29.2	164.0
Calcium	1.0	3.0	6.1	16	34.9	162.7
Magnesium	1.6	4.8	1.6	0	4.8	20.0
Sodium	0.4	1.2	1.8	10	5.3	29.8
Potassium	1.5	4.5	1.1	0	2.2	9.4
Chloride	0.8	2.4	1.2	0	1.5	6.8
Nitrate	0.16	0.48	0.51	6	<0.16	2.6
Sulfate	1.0	3.0	1.0	0	7.6	52.0

[1]Detection limits from http://www.fs.fed.us/air/documents/LabBrochureRevised_1_3_08.pdf, accessed May 2011.

in some samples. Given the concentration range observed in the environmental samples (table 2), however, this level of bias should have a minimal effect on the interpretation of the calcium and sodium data. The overlap of nitrate concentrations in field blanks and environmental samples might indicate a small positive bias in the environmental nitrate data. Based on the field replicate samples at selected sites, reproducibility of ANC, calcium, magnesium, sodium, potassium, and sulfate is better than ±15 percent, indicating replicate analyses are within analytical uncertainty. The variability in chloride and nitrate concentrations between replicates was slightly higher (±25 percent), reflecting the fact that concentrations of chloride and nitrate in the environmental samples are closer to the ARML detection limits compared to other constituents (table 2).

Trends in lake-water concentrations during the summer months (mid-June to mid-September) were calculated using the Mann-Kendall test with Sen slope estimator. There are no streamflow-monitoring stations at or near the study lakes, so the lake-water concentrations could not be corrected for hydrologic conditions prior to trend analysis. Changes in analytical methods and laboratories that occurred during the study period were evaluated to ensure the comparability of the data over the study period. The lakes selected for analyses had at least 10 samples that were collected over a minimum period of record of 14 years. The exceptions were two lakes in Idaho (sites 2 and 3) and three lakes in Utah (sites 15–17), which had as few as eight samples and less than 10 years of record. Despite the limited records, these lakes were retained in the analysis because they are the only available lake-chemistry data for these wilderness areas and results are included in the tables and figures of this report.

Trends in Emissions and Atmospheric Deposition in the Rocky Mountain Region

Emissions from anthropogenic activities are the main sources of sulfur and nitrogen pollutants reaching remote aquatic ecosystems in the Rocky Mountain region (Baron and Denning, 1993; Peterson and others, 1998; Burns, 2004). Deposition of pollutants occurs both by wet (rain and snow) and dry (accumulation of particles and gases) processes, although dry deposition is estimated to account for less than 25 percent of total sulfur and nitrogen deposition in the Western United States (U.S. Environmental Protection Agency, 2008). One way to evaluate the effect of anthropogenic emissions on the environment is with atmospheric monitoring networks that provide long-term consistent data that can be used to track temporal and spatial trends in regional air quality (Nilles, 2000). Such assessments are important to scientists, resource managers, and policymakers for evaluating the effectiveness of regulatory actions on improving the water quality of precipitation and surface water. This section examines trends in emissions of sulfur and nitrogen compounds in the Rocky Mountain region using data from the USEPA National Emissions Inventory. Emissions data were obtained from the USEPA National Emissions Inventory [(NEI) at *http://www.epa.gov/air/data/*, accessed May 2011]. In addition, this section examines spatial patterns and trends in the chemistry of atmospheric deposition for 23 wet-deposition stations, 48 snowpack monitoring sites, and 8 dry deposition stations in Colorado, Montana, Utah, and Wyoming.

Emissions

SO$_2$ emissions in the United States are highest in the Midwest, Southeast, and Texas (fig. 6) with 65 percent of emissions coming from just 12 States in these regions. By comparison, emissions in the Western United States are quite low with seven States in the Rocky Mountain region (Arizona, Colorado, Idaho, Montana, New Mexico, Utah, and Wyoming) accounting for about 3 percent of national SO$_2$ emissions in 2005 (fig. 6). The United States has experienced more than a 50-percent reduction in SO$_2$ emissions from large stationary sources over the past several decades, largely as a result of the 1990 Clean Air Act Amendments (Stoddard and others, 2003). In the Rocky Mountain region, SO$_2$ emissions from large stationary sources (*http://www.epa.gov/airmarkets/*, accessed May 2011) have followed a similar trend, decreasing by 46 percent since the mid-1990s (fig. 7). Decreasing SO$_2$ emissions in the Rocky Mountains likely have resulted from emission reductions at a few large coal-fired powerplants. In Colorado, for example, about one-half of the SO$_2$ reductions for the State are the result of emission controls retrofitted at the Craig and Hayden powerplants (fig. 3) in northwestern Colorado (Colorado Department of Public Health and Environment, 2007). Similarly in Arizona, 80 percent of SO$_2$ reductions are related to installation of SO$_2$ scrubbers at the Navajo Generating Station (fig. 3) in northern Arizona in the late 1990s (Green and others, 2005).

NO$_x$ emissions across the United States show a slightly different spatial pattern than SO$_2$ (fig. 6) due to substantial contributions from mobile and nonpoint sources such as vehicle emissions, oil and gas exploration and production activities, and agricultural activities. Based on the 2005 NEI, nonpoint sources in the United States account for 70 percent of annual NO$_x$ emissions compared to 19 percent for SO$_2$ (*http://www.epa.gov/air/data/*, accessed May 2011). In the Rocky Mountain region, NO$_x$ from nonpoint sources accounts for 60 percent of annual emissions, ranging from 36 percent in Wyoming to as much as 91 percent in Idaho. For the entire United States, NO$_x$ emissions from large point sources declined by 50 percent since 1995, but in the Rocky Mountain region declines have been more modest at about 25 percent (fig. 7). Based on the NEI, NO$_x$ emissions from nonpoint sources in the Rocky Mountain region have decreased by about 30 percent since 1995 with most of the decrease occurring since 2000 (*http://www.epa.gov/air/data/*, accessed May 2011).

Ammonia (NH$_3$) emissions primarily result from agricultural activities with the largest contribution from livestock operations and fertilizer applications; however, there remain large uncertainties in the magnitude of these emissions Z-(U.S. Environmental Protection Agency, 2004). NH$_3$ emissions in the Rocky Mountain States accounted for about 9 percent of annual emissions in the United States and were highest in northeastern Colorado and central and southern Idaho. Available data from NEI indicate that NH$_3$ emissions in the Rocky Mountain region have decreased slightly over the period 1996 to 2005 (*http://www.epa.gov/air/data/*, accessed

May 2011); however, there is a high degree of uncertainty associated with NH$_3$ emissions inventories and the apparent trends in emissions may not be reliable.

Trends in Precipitation Chemistry

Decreases in sulfate concentrations in wet deposition were observed across the Rocky Mountain region over the period 1988 to 2008 (table 3, fig. 8). Statistically significant (p-value less than or equal to 0.05) downward trends in sulfate were detected at 21 of the 23 stations with the largest decreases for stations in Colorado and Utah (table 3). Percent declines at individual NADP stations ranged from 22 to 65 percent and averaged 43 percent, which is similar to the total reduction in SO$_2$ emissions of 46 percent for the Rocky Mountain region, indicating that precipitation chemistry is responding to regional changes in air quality. This result is consistent with studies in the Eastern United States that have attributed changes in precipitation chemistry to emissions reductions established under the 1990 Clean Air Act Amendments (Driscoll and others, 2003; Stoddard and others, 2003; Burns and others, 2006). Because SO$_2$ is converted to sulfuric acid in the atmosphere, the expectation is that declines in sulfate should be accompanied by declines in precipitation acidity (Stoddard and others, 2003). At 15 of the 23 stations, there were significant decreases in hydrogen-ion concentrations that, on an equivalents basis, roughly balanced the decreases in sulfate for most of the stations (table 3). The lack of correspondence at some stations might in part be related to neutralization of acidity in the atmosphere by reaction with mineral dust. Alternatively, the use of estimated hydrogen-ion concentrations (2004 to 2008) in the trend analysis could have had some effect on the resulting trends.

The largest downward trends in precipitation sulfate in the study area were measured at Murphy Ridge station (UT08), located near the Utah–Wyoming State line, and the Dry Lake (CO93) and Summit Lake (CO97) stations in northern Colorado (fig. 3). Murphy Ridge is about 80 miles northeast of the Kennecott Copper Corporation, where substantial reductions in SO$_2$ emissions resulted following implementation of a new smelting process that came online in 1995 (*http://www.airquality.utah.gov/Public-Interest/about_pollutants/about_sulfurdioxde.htm*, accessed May 2011). The two Colorado NADP stations are within 50 miles of the Craig and Hayden powerplants (Mast and others, 2005). Emissions control units were installed during 1998–99 at Hayden and during 2003–04 at Craig, which reduced SO$_2$ emissions by more than 90 percent (Colorado Department of Public Health and Environment, 2007). Because the powerplants are immediately upwind of these NADP stations, changes in emissions from those plants appeared to have a more pronounced effect on the precipitation chemistry at those stations compared to more distant stations.

Trends in nitrogen species (nitrate and ammonium) were not as widespread as those observed for sulfate (fig. 8). Trends

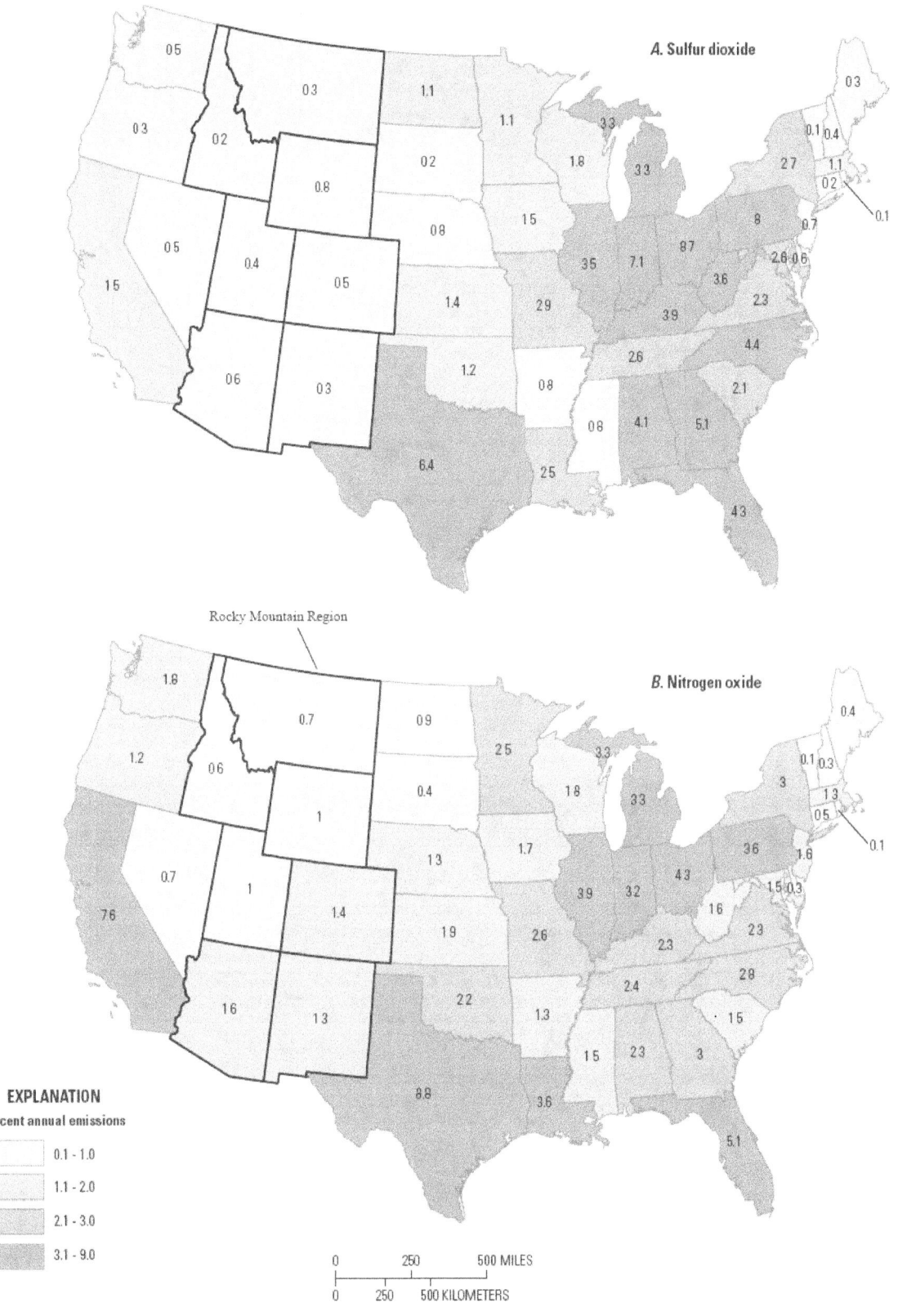

Figure 6. Percentage of (*A*) annual sulfur dioxide (SO₂) and (*B*) nitrogen oxide (NOₓ) emissions by State in the continental United States during 2005 (data source: *http://www.epa.gov/air/data/*, accessed May 2011).

Table 3. Trends in monthly precipitation-weighted mean concentrations and annual precipitation amount at 23 National Atmospheric Deposition Program (NADP) stations in the Rocky Mountain region for 1988 to 2008

[Station no., station number from figure 3; Spec. cond., specific conductance in microsiemens per centimeter per year; Precip., precipitation amount in inches per year; trends for other constituents in microequivalents per liter per year; --, trend not statistically significant; dark blue shading indicates downward trend with p-value less than or equal to 0.01; light blue shading indicates downward trend with p-value greater than 0.01 and less than or equal to 0.05; dark orange shading indicates upward trend with p-value less than or equal to 0.01; light orange shading indicates upward trend with p-value greater than 0.01 and less than or equal to 0.05]

Station no.	Station name	Spec. cond.	Hydrogen	Calcium	Magnesium	Potassium	Sodium	Ammonium	Nitrate	Chloride	Sulfate	Precip.
CO00	Alamosa	--	--	--		--	-0.14	0.22	--	-0.08	-0.24	--
CO02	Niwot Saddle	--	--	0.14		--	-0.10	0.19	--	-0.06	-0.18	--
CO08	Four Mile Park	--	-0.17	--		--	-0.10	--		-0.08	-0.23	--
CO19	Beaver Meadows	--	-0.28	--		--	-0.09	0.27		-0.06	-0.18	--
CO21	Manitou	--	--	--		--	-0.09	0.34		-0.06	-0.15	--
CO91[1]	Wolf Creek Pass	-0.11	--	0.22		0.01	--	0.14		--	-0.21	--
CO92	Sunlight Peak	--	--	--			-0.10			-0.08	-0.23	--
CO93	Dry Lake	-0.21	-0.49	--	-0.03		-0.08		-0.20	-0.07	-0.57	--
CO94	Sugarloaf	-0.07	-0.21	--			-0.08			-0.05	-0.33	--
CO96	Molas Pass	-0.07		--			-0.08			-0.06	-0.23	--
CO97	Summit Lake	-0.13	-0.40	--			-0.09	0.18		-0.07	-0.50	--
CO98	Loch Vale	--	-0.20	0.08	-0.01	0.01	-0.08	0.10		-0.05	-0.18	--
MT05	Glacier National Park	--	-0.16	--			-0.08	0.15		-0.04	-0.15	--
MT07	Clancy	--	-0.19	--		0.01	-0.08	--		-0.05	-0.20	--
MT97[1]	Lost Trail Pass	--	-0.15	--			-0.05	--		-0.02	--	--
UT08	Murphy Ridge	-0.21	--	--	-0.06		-0.23	--		-0.22	-0.45	--
WY00	Snowy Range	--	-0.16	--			-0.12	0.18		-0.08	-0.21	--
WY02	Sinks Canyon	--	-0.27	--			-0.09	0.18		-0.06	-0.20	--
WY06	Pinedale	--		--			-0.12	--		-0.08	-0.20	--
WY08	Tower Falls	--	-0.10	--	-0.02		-0.08	0.19		-0.07	--	--
WY95[1]	Brooklyn Lake	-0.08	-0.29	--			-0.11	0.16		-0.06	-0.16	--
WY97	South Pass City	--	-0.36	--		0.01	--	--		-0.08	-0.15	--
WY98	Gypsum Creek	-0.05	-0.17	--			-0.14	0.10		-0.12	-0.1	--

[1]Trends were computed from 1991–2008 for CO91 and 1993–2008 for MT97 and WY95.

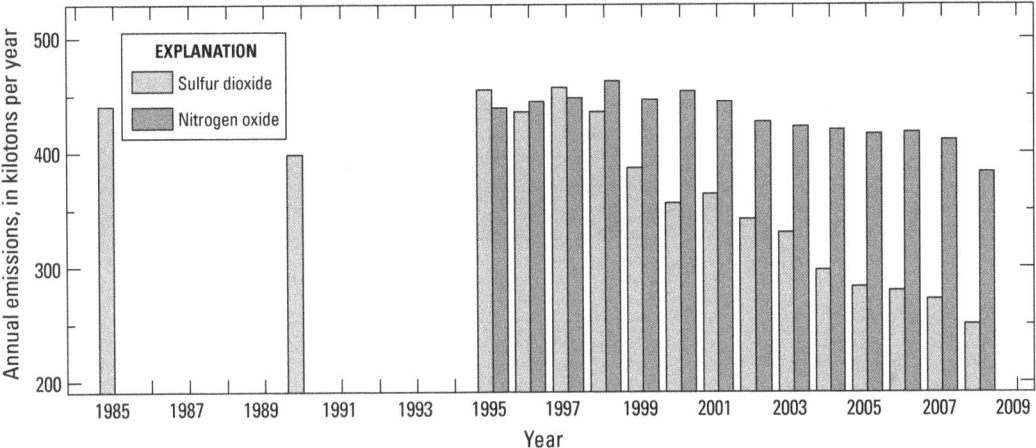

Figure 7. Trends in sulfur dioxide (SO_2) and nitrogen oxide (NO_x) emissions from large stationary sources in seven States in the Rocky Mountain region including Arizona, Colorado, Idaho, Montana, New Mexico, Utah, and Wyoming (data source: *http://www.epa.gov/air/data/*, accessed May 2011).

in nitrate generally were not statistically significant; only the Dry Lake station (CO93) showed a weak downward trend of –0.20 microequivalents per liter per year (μeq/L/yr) (table 3). The lack of trends does not appear to be consistent with the NEI data set, which indicates a modest decline in NO_x emissions in the Rocky Mountain region since the mid-1990s. Significant upward trends in ammonium concentrations ranging from +0.10 to +0.34 μeq/L/yr were detected at 13 of the 23 stations (table 3). The results are consistent with Lehman and others (2007) who reported nationwide increases in ammonium concentrations at NADP stations for the period 1985 to 2004. Most of the increase in ammonium concentrations in the Rocky Mountain region occurred after 1998 (fig. 8) and was strongest at NADP stations east of the Continental Divide particularly stations in Colorado (CO02, CO19, CO21, CO98) that are closest to agricultural and urban areas in the eastern part of the state (fig. 3). Available NEI data indicate NH_3 emissions were fairly constant from 1996 to 2000 then dropped in 2001 and 2002, which is inconsistent with observed ammonium trends at NADP stations. Lehmann and others (2007) noted the same inconsistency with NH_3 emissions and suggested increases in ratios of ammonium to sulfate greater than one might account for some of the observed ammonium increases. An excess of ammonium over sulfate reduces the transport distance leading to greater deposition from local sources (Hov and Hjøllo, 1994). For the Rocky Mountain region, ammonium to sulfate ratios at NADP stations rose rapidly after 2000 (fig. 8) creating an ammonium-rich environment that might have contributed to enhanced local deposition in some areas. This increase in ratios might partially explain why trends were greatest at sites closest to source areas in eastern Colorado despite the fact that regional NH_3 emissions appear to have decreased since 2001. These results suggest that decreases in SO_2 emissions may be contributing to enhanced ammonium deposition in some high-elevation areas of the Rocky Mountains.

Trends in base-cation concentrations were detected at only a few NADP stations, with the exception of sodium, which showed strong downward trends at 21 of 23 stations. Similar trends were observed for chloride although they tended to be slightly smaller in magnitude (table 3). Visual inspection of annual sodium concentrations in the study area indicates that most of the decrease in sodium occurred before 1998 (fig. 8). There were several changes in NADP protocols that might have affected sodium and perhaps chloride concentrations, including contamination from the bucket lid before 1994 and contamination from filters used before 1998 (*http://nadp.sws.uiuc.edu/QA/*, accessed May 2011). Wetherbee and others (2009) reported a positive bias in weekly sodium concentrations when comparing 1986–93 data for NADP to a Canadian precipitation network and concluded that it likely was due to NADP 1994 sampling and 1998 filtering-protocol changes. A recent analysis of the entire NADP data set reported downward trends in sodium and chloride at 90 percent of the stations over the period 1984 to 2006 (Lloyd, 2010). Lloyd (2010) could not identify the cause of the trends but suggested they may be related to climate change.

Trends in Snowpack and Winter-Wetfall Chemistry

Although NADP wet-deposition stations provide year-around monitoring throughout much of the region and offer long-term records and comparisons for 250 sites nationally, high-elevation stations are sparse. The RMSN maintains a substantially greater geographic coverage of the Rocky Mountains (fig. 3). The high-elevation snowpack is important because it accumulates 2–3 times the annual precipitation measured at lower elevations where regular monitoring is more easily accomplished and more commonly done. Further, snowpacks afford a more complete analysis of wintertime deposition by

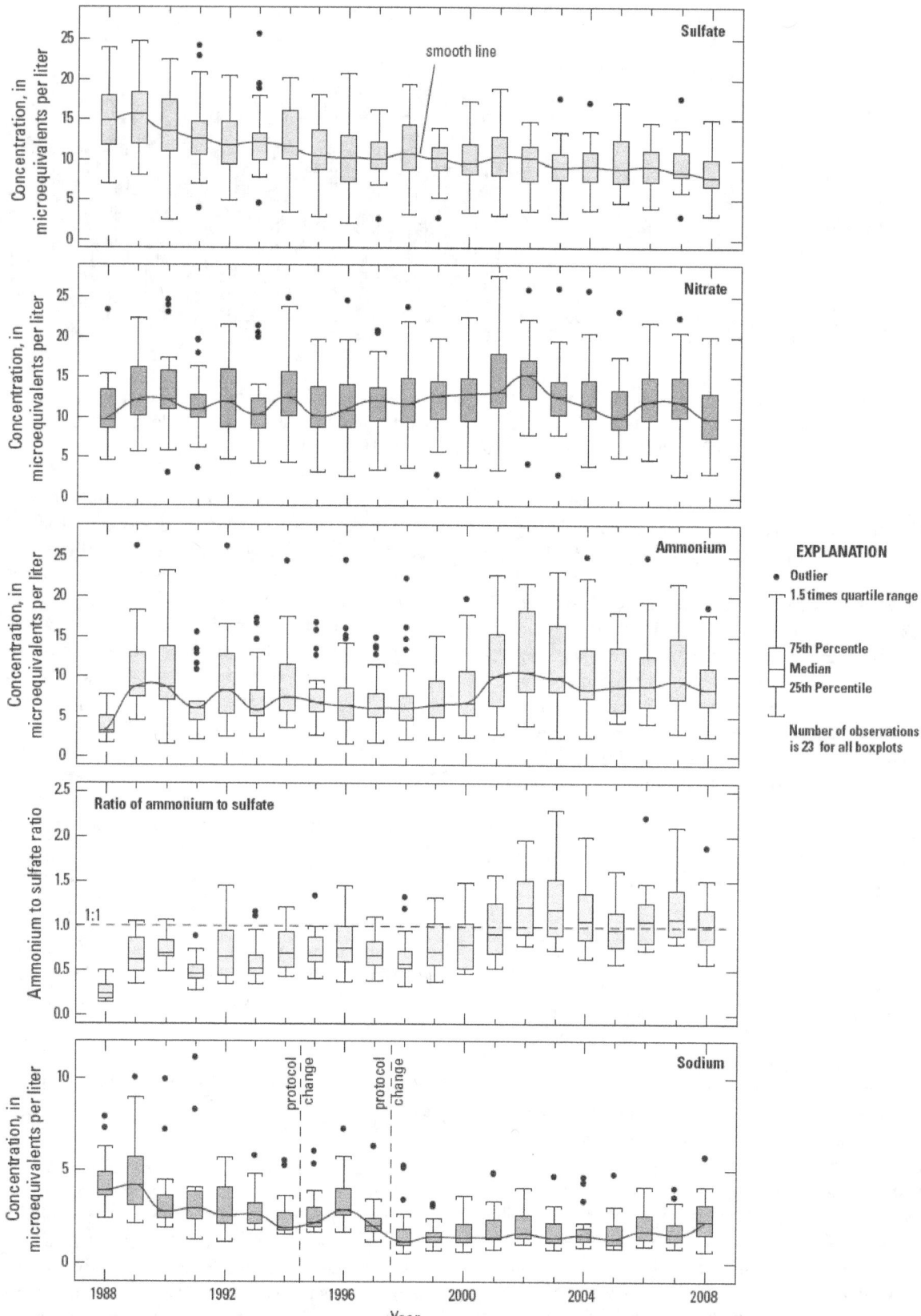

Figure 8.   Trends in annual volume-weighted mean concentrations of sulfate, nitrate, ammonium, ammonium to sulfate ratio, and sodium in wet deposition at 23 National Atmospheric Deposition Program (NADP) stations in the Rocky Mountain region from 1988 to 2008.

capturing both wet and dry deposition [dry nitrogen and sulfur deposition accounts for as much as 25 percent of total annual deposition (U.S. Environmental Protection Agency, 2008)]. In this section, results of tests for trends in concentrations of ammonium, calcium, hydrogen, nitrate, and sulfate are compared for snowpack (RMSN) and winter-only wetfall (November–April; herein called wetfall) (NADP). Comparisons of regional, subregional, and local assessments are discussed and are also compared to other work in the Rocky Mountain region.

At the regional scale, significant trends in chemical concentrations of ammonium, calcium, hydrogen, and sulfate for both the snowpack and the wetfall networks were observed for the period 1993–2008 (table 4). For both networks, ammonium and calcium concentrations showed significant upward trends for the period, and hydrogen and sulfate concentrations showed significant downward trends. No trends were observed at the regional scale for nitrate concentrations in snowpack or wetfall. Regional trends in ammonium concentrations in snowpacks generally are consistent with those for wetfall. The significant upward trends in calcium concentrations are consistent with observations of recent dust storms and red-dust deposition (Neff and others, 2008; Clow and others, 2009). Downward trends in sulfate concentrations are consistent with regional declines in SO_2 emissions in the region (fig. 7).

At the subregional scale, significant trends in both snowpack and wetfall concentrations also were observed, but differences in concentration patterns among subregions are apparent (table 4). In the Northern Rockies subregion, there were only two regional trends, with an upward trend in wetfall calcium concentrations and a downward trend in snowpack sulfate concentrations. Such limited changes in concentrations over time might reflect the relatively sparse population density in this subregion of the Rocky Mountains.

In the Central Rockies subregion, significant upward trends in snowpack concentrations were observed for both ammonium and calcium concentrations, whereas significant downward trends were observed in hydrogen and sulfate concentrations. No trends were observed for snowpack nitrate concentrations. Upward trends in ammonium and calcium concentrations in snowpacks may reflect land-use practices, which result in increased agricultural emissions of ammonia and generation of dust available for eolian transport. In contrast to the snowpack chemistry, no trends were observed in wetfall chemistry for any of the five constituents. This disparity between the snowpack and wetfall chemistry in the Central Rockies subregion may be due to the sparse number (2) of wetfall stations representing this subregion, but the disparity also may due to the exclusion of dry deposition in samples collected at wetfall sites. Dry deposition can account for as much as 25 percent of total deposition (wet plus dry) in the Rocky Mountain region (U.S. Environmental Protection Agency, 2008).

In the Southern Rockies subregion, where NADP wetfall stations are more numerous (12), trends for the two networks compared more closely. For both snowpack and wetfall chemistry, highly significant upward trends were seen for calcium, and highly significant downward trends were observed for hydrogen and for sulfate. The upward trends in calcium concentrations observed for both networks likely are associated with several windblown dust events observed in recent years (Clow and others, 2009). This effect is more likely to cause increases of calcium in the Southern Rockies subregion due to its proximity to sources of calcium-bearing dust in desert regions of neighboring States including Arizona, New Mexico, and Utah. A slight upward trend in snowpack nitrate concentrations was observed, but there was no trend in wetfall nitrate concentrations.

At the local scale, trends in concentrations for individual snowpack sites and wetfall stations provided the basis for

Table 4.   Regional and subregional trends in snowpack and winter-only (November–April) wetfall concentrations in the Rocky Mountain region for 1993 to 2008.

[Trends in microequivalents per liter per year; --, trend not statistically significant; dark blue shading indicates downward trend with p-value less than or equal to 0.01; light blue shading indicates downward trend with p-value greater than 0.01 and less than or equal to 0.05; dark orange shading indicates upward trend with p-value less than or equal to 0.01; light orange shading indicates upward trend with p-value greater than 0.01 and less than or equal to 0.05]

Type of site	Number of sites	Ammonium	Calcium	Hydrogen	Nitrate	Sulfate
Regional trends						
Snowpack	48	0.044	0.14	−0.2	--	−0.12
Winter wetfall	17	0.05	0.18	−0.15	--	−0.18
Subregional trends: Northern Rocky Mountains						
Snowpack	7	--	--	--	--	−0.07
Winter wetfall	3	--	0.10	--	--	--
Subregional trends: Central Rocky Mountains						
Snowpack	17	0.10	0.03	−0.17	--	−0.11
Winter wetfall	2	--	--	--	--	--
Subregional trends: Southern Rocky Mountains						
Snowpack	24	--	0.41	−0.32	0.06	−0.14
Winter wetfall	12	--	0.26	−0.19	--	−0.21

calculations of regional and subregional trends. In many cases, observed positive or negative trends in concentrations during the study at individual snowpack sites and wetfall stations (table 5 and fig. 9) were consistent with regional and subregional trends, but not always. For example, only 2 out of 48 stations showed upward trends in ammonium, yet when snowpack sites were analyzed as a group, significant upward trends in ammonium were detected for the Rocky Mountain region (table 4). Few significant trends were observed at individual sites or stations in the Northern Rockies subregion. Individual trends in the Central Rockies subregion also were sparse compared to those seen in the Southern Rockies subregion, where more anthropogenic activity occurs and there is more exposure to the desert areas of neighboring States. Accordingly, nearly one-half of the snowpack sites and wetfall stations in the Southern Rockies subregion showed significant trends in concentrations of calcium (upward), hydrogen (downward), or sulfate (downward). Regional and subregional trends mentioned herein agree with these individual trends for these three constituents, but not for ammonium and nitrate. At all locations in both networks across all three subregions, only two significant trends were observed for ammonium and none were observed for nitrate. Yet, upward regional or subregional trends were reported for ammonium and nitrate in table 4. This was due to the aggregate effects that numerous, statistically insignificant, individual patterns of increasing concentrations have on the RKT results for both ammonium and nitrate concentrations (Helsel and Frans, 2006). For example, although tests of individual snowpack sites in the Southern Rockies subregion showed no significant trends in nitrate concentrations, the RKT result for that subregion showed a significant ($p<0.03$) upward trend of 0.06 microequivalent of nitrate per liter per year (table 4) largely because 79 percent of the 24 snowpack sites in that subregion had positive, yet statistically insignificant ($p>0.05$), slopes for nitrate concentrations. This same basic relation was observed for ammonium concentrations. Thus, the upward regional and subregional trends indicated here for ammonium and nitrate concentrations in snowpack and winter wetfall are statistically valid. However, the environmental significance of such a small regional or subregional increase in concentrations per year may be minor.

In summary, comparisons of snowpack and wetfall chemistry for ammonium, calcium, hydrogen, nitrate, and sulfate are in general agreement, and trends and other patterns in those data generally are consistent with other regional work regarding atmospheric emissions. The limited occurrence of upward trends in chemical concentrations of ammonium and nitrate in snowpacks and wetfall in the Rocky Mountain region indicates minor environmental significance at both regional and subregional scales; however, there may be more environmental concern with patterns in calcium concentrations. Significant upward trends in calcium concentrations in both snowpacks and wetfall in the Southern Rockies subregion support the assertion that the proximity to arid landscapes to the south and west has a positive effect on calcium concentrations. Continued

increases in calcium concentrations in snowpacks and wetfall resulting from increased dust accumulation on snow may contribute to undesirable long-term consequences including earlier-than-normal snowmelt runoff (Clow and others, 2009). In contrast, significant downward trends in hydrogen and sulfate concentrations at nearly one-half the snowpack sites and wetfall stations in the Southern Rockies subregion clearly indicate improving conditions with less atmospheric deposition of acidic pollutants. This is noteworthy in a region of increasing population and energy development.

Trends in Dry Deposition Chemistry

Trends in concentrations of gaseous and particulate sulfur and nitrogen compounds were determined for eight CAST-NET stations in the Rocky Mountains; seven of the stations are in mountainous areas and one is in the desert (CAN407). Because dry deposition is more difficult and expensive to measure than wet deposition, CASTNET stations are more sparsely located and generally at lower elevations compared to other deposition stations discussed in this report. Trends at the CASTNET stations are in agreement with trends in SO_2 emissions in the Rocky Mountain region. Trends in SO_2 concentrations are downward and statistically significant at six of the eight stations (table 6). The largest trends were at Canyonlands (CAN407) and Mesa Verde (MEV405), which seems reasonable given the proximity of these sites to the Navajo Generating station and Four Corners powerplants (fig. 3), which have experienced substantial declines in emissions since the mid-1990s (Green and others, 2005). Downward trends in particulate sulfate concentrations also were detected at four of the stations showing trends in SO_2 (table 6).

For nitrogen compounds, only two out of eight stations showed trends in nitrate species (NO_3 and HNO_3), which is consistent with the lack of trends at NADP stations but inconsistent with declines in NO_x emissions indicated by the NEI. The two stations that did show upward trends in HNO_3 (MEV405 and PND165) are located in areas of the Rocky Mountains that are experiencing rapid development of oil and gas resources (Eastern Research Group, Inc., 2006). Drilling rig and compressor engines associated with these activities have been reported to be substantial sources of NO_x emissions in the region (Eastern Research Group, Inc., 2006). Interestingly, an upward trend in NO_3 was not detected at the WY06 NADP station (table 3), which is colocated with the PND165 CASTNET station (table 6). Particulate ammonium showed weak downward trends at three of the six CASTNET stations. Although this is consistent with slight downward trends in NH_3 emissions from NEI, it is opposite to the trend pattern observed for ammonium concentrations at many of the NADP stations (table 3).

Table 5. Trends in winter-only concentrations measured at 48 snowpack sites and 17 winter wetfall stations in the Rocky Mountain region for 1993 to 2008.

[Site/station no., site/station number from figure 3; trends in microequivalents per liter per year; --, trend not statistically significant; light blue shading indicates downward trend with p-value greater than 0.01 and less than or equal to 0.05; dark orange shading indicates upward trend with p-value less than or equal to 0.01; light orange shading indicates upward trend with p-value greater than 0.01 and less than or equal to 0.05]

Site/station no.	Type of site/ station	Site name	Ammonium	Calcium	Hydrogen	Nitrate	Sulfate
		Northern Rocky Mountains					
1	snowpack	Big Mountain, Mont.	--	--	--	--	−0.13
2	snowpack	Chief Joseph Pass, Mont.	--	--	--	--	--
3	snowpack	Granite Pass, Mont.	--	--	--	--	--
4	snowpack	Kings Hill, Mont.	--	--	--	--	--
5	snowpack	Noisy Basin, Mont.	--	--	--	--	--
6	snowpack	Red Mountain, Mont.	--	0.34	--	--	--
7	snowpack	Snow Bowl, Mont.	--	--	--	--	--
MT05	winter wetfall	Glacier Park, Mont.	--	--	--	--	--
MT07	winter wetfall	Clancy, Mont.	--	--	--	--	--
MT97	winter wetfall	Lost Trail, Mont.	--	0.13	--	--	--
		Central Rocky Mountains					
8	snowpack	Big Sky, Mont.	--	--	--	--	--
9	snowpack	Canyon, Wyo.	--	--	--	--	--
10	snowpack	Daisy Pass, Mont.	--	--	--	--	--
11	snowpack	Elkhart Park, Wyo.	--	--	--	--	−0.14
12	snowpack	Four Mile Meadow, Wyo.	--	--	--	--	--
13	snowpack	Garnet Canyon, Wyo.	0.22	0.35	−0.31	--	--
14	snowpack	Gypsum Creek, Wyo.	--	--	−0.18	--	--
15	snowpack	Lewis Lake Divide, Wyo.	--	0.03	--	--	--
16	snowpack	Lionshead, Mont.	--	--	--	--	−0.3
17	snowpack	Old Faithful, Wyo.	--	--	--	--	--
18	snowpack	Rendezvous Mountain, Wyo.	0.22	--	--	--	--
19	snowpack	South Pass, Wyo.	--	--	--	--	--
20	snowpack	Sylvan Lake, Wyo.	--	--	−0.22	--	--
21	snowpack	Teton Pass, Wyo.	--	--	--	--	--
22	snowpack	Togwotee Pass, Wyo.	--	--	--	--	--
23	snowpack	Twenty-one Mile, Mont.	--	--	−0.31	--	−0.19
24	snowpack	West Yellowstone, Mont.	--	--	--	--	--
WY97	winter wetfall	South Pass, Wyo.	--	--	--	--	--
WY98	winter wetfall	Gypsum Creek, Wyo.	--	--	--	--	--

Table 5. Trends in winter-only concentrations measured at 48 snowpack sites and 17 winter wetfall stations in the Rocky Mountain region for 1993 to 2008.—Continued

[Site/station no., site/station number from figure 3; trends in microequivalents per liter per year; --, trend not statistically significant; dark blue shading indicates downward trend with p-value less than or equal to 0.01; light blue shading indicates downward trend with p-value greater than 0.01 and less than or equal to 0.05; dark orange shading indicates upward trend with p-value less than or equal to 0.01; light orange shading indicates upward trend with p-value greater than 0.01 and less than or equal to 0.05]

Site/station no.	Type of site/ station	Site name	Ammonium	Calcium	Hydrogen	Nitrate	Sulfate
			Southern Rocky Mountains				
25	snowpack	Berthoud Pass, Colo.	--	0.47	−0.23	--	--
26	snowpack	Brooklyn Lake, Wyo.	--	0.41	−0.42	--	--
27	snowpack	Brumley, Colo.	--	0.54	--	--	--
28	snowpack	Buffalo Pass, Colo.	--	--	--	--	−0.34
29	snowpack	Cameron Pass, Colo.	--	--	--	--	−0.21
30	snowpack	Divide Peak, Wyo.	--	0.80	−0.48	--	--
31	snowpack	Dry Lake, Colo.	--	0.19	−0.67	--	−0.49
32	snowpack	Dunckley Pass, Colo.	--	--	−0.27	--	−0.11
33	snowpack	Elk River, Colo.	--	0.59	−0.68	--	--
34	snowpack	Fremont Pass, Colo.	--	--	--	--	--
35	snowpack	Grand Mesa, Colo.	--	--	−0.38	--	--
36	snowpack	Hopewell, N.Mex.	--	--	--	--	--
37	snowpack	Lake Irene, Colo.	--	0.39	−0.45	--	--
38	snowpack	Loch Vale, Colo.	--	--	−0.53	--	−0.26
39	snowpack	Loveland Pass, Colo.	--	--	--	--	--
40	snowpack	Molas Lake, Colo.	--	--	--	--	--
41	snowpack	Monarch Pass, Colo.	--	--	--	--	--
42	snowpack	Old Battle, Wyo.	--	0.36	--	--	−0.22
43	snowpack	Rabbit Ears 1, Colo.	--	--	−0.63	--	−0.31
44	snowpack	Red Mountain Pass, Colo.	--	--	--	--	--
45	snowpack	Slumgullion Pass, Colo.	--	--	--	--	−0.12
46	snowpack	Sunlight Peak, Colo.	--	--	--	--	−0.09
47	snowpack	University Camp, Colo.	--	--	−0.46	--	--
48	snowpack	Wolf Creek Pass, Colo.	--	--	--	--	--
CO02	winter wetfall	Niwot Saddle, Colo.	--	--	--	--	--
CO08	winter wetfall	Four Mile Park, Colo.	--	--	--	--	−0.14
CO19	winter wetfall	Beaver Meadows, Colo.	--	0.35	--	--	--
CO91	winter wetfall	Wolf Creek Pass, Colo.	--	--	−0.25	--	−0.47
CO92	winter wetfall	Sunlight Peak, Colo.	--	--	--	--	−0.18
CO93	winter wetfall	Dry Lake, Colo.	--	--	−0.35	--	−0.55
CO94	winter wetfall	Sugarloaf, Colo.	--	--	--	--	−0.24
CO96	winter wetfall	Molas Pass, Colo.	--	--	--	--	−0.21
CO97	winter wetfall	Buffalo Pass, Colo.	--	--	−0.31	--	−0.58
CO98	winter wetfall	Loch Vale, Colo.	--	--	--	--	--
WY00	winter wetfall	Snowy Range, Wyo.	--	0.49	--	--	--
WY95	winter wetfall	Brooklyn Lake, Wyo.	--	0.20	--	--	--

Summary of Emission and Deposition Trends

Data from available emission inventories indicate substantial reductions in SO$_2$ emissions have occurred in the Rocky Mountain region since the mid-1990s as a result of emissions controls placed on large powerplants. Annual NO$_x$ and NH$_3$ emissions in the Rocky Mountains over the same period also declined, however, there is a high degree of uncertainty associated with emissions inventories from nonpoint sources and the apparent trends in nitrogen emissions may not be reliable (U.S. Environmental Protection Agency, 2004). Considering the dominant sources of sulfur and nitrogen emissions in the Rocky Mountains, there is greater potential for future increases in nitrogen than sulfur emissions. Recent predictions by Western Regional Air Partnership (WRAP) estimate that SO$_2$ emissions in the western United States will increase by 20 percent by 2018 compared to an increase of more than a 50 percent increase for NO$_x$ (Eastern Research Group, Inc., 2006). WRAP estimates for NH$_3$ emissions in 2018 remain unchanged relative to 2002 inventories. The large increases in NO$_x$ emissions for 2018 (more than doubling in New Mexico and Wyoming) primarily result from large projected increases in oil and gas production activity in the Rocky Mountain region.

Trends in deposition data from all three monitoring networks (NADP, RMSN, and CASTNET) are consistent with decreases in SO$_2$ emissions, indicating that that emission controls have improved deposition chemistry in the region. Considering sources of SO$_2$ emissions, future increases in sulfate deposition should be minimal, which should reduce the risk of acidification caused by SO$_2$ to high-elevation aquatic ecosystems. The picture for nitrogen deposition is not the same; nitrate in wet deposition has remained relatively constant while increases in ammonium were observed at many of the monitoring stations, indicating that inorganic nitrogen deposition has leveled off or increased slightly in the region. These trends are inconsistent with available emission inventories that indicate that modest reductions in both NO$_x$ and NH$_3$ emissions have occurred over a similar period of record. This discrepancy may reflect uncertainties in the emission inventories or that there have been changes in the atmospheric transformations of nitrogen species that may be affecting deposition processes (Lehman and others, 2007). Considering the potential for future increases in oil and gas production in the Rocky Mountains, nitrogen deposition may continue to pose a risk to aquatic ecosystems from both acidification and nitrification.

Trends in Climate Variables in the Rocky Mountain Region

Although there is growing evidence that the global climate is warming due to anthropogenic emissions of greenhouse gases (Intergovernmental Panel on Climate Change, 2007), the effect of anthropogenic forcings on climate and ecosystems in high-elevation areas of the Rocky Mountain region is only beginning to be understood (Baron and others, 2009; Clow, 2010; Rangwala and Miller, 2010). This section examines changes in climate in the study area by analyzing trends in minimum (T$_{min}$) and maximum (T$_{max}$) air temperatures and precipitation amount at selected SNOTEL stations over the period 1990 to 2006.

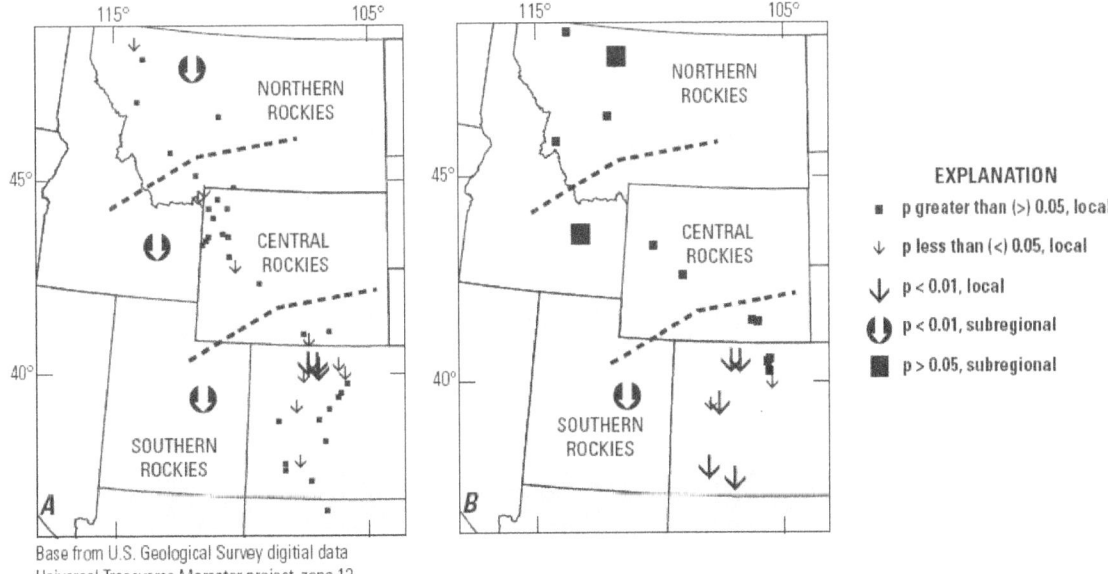

Base from U.S. Geological Survey digitial data
Universal Transverse Mercator project, zone 13

Figure 9. Subregional and individual trends in sulfate concentrations in (A) snowpack and (B) winter-only wetfall in the Rocky Mountain region for 1993 to 2008.

Table 6. Trends in concentrations of sulfur and nitrogen species measured at eight dry deposition stations in the Clean Air Status and Trends Network (CASTNET) for 1989 to 2008.

[Station no, station number from figure 3; Elevation above North American Vertical Datum of 1988; NH_4, ammonium; NO_3, nitrate; HNO_3, nitric acid; SO_2, sulfur dioxide; SO_4, sulfate; ng/cm³, nanograms per cubic centimeter; --, trend not significant; dark blue shading indicates downward trend with p-value less than or equal to 0.01; light blue shading indicates downward trend with p-value greater than 0.01 and less than or equal to 0.05; dark orange shading indicates upward trend with p-value less than or equal to 0.01; light orange shading indicates upward trend with p-value greater than 0.01 and less than or equal to 0.05; <, less than; NP, National Park]

Station no.	Station name	Elevation (feet)	Land use	Particulate NH_4 (ng/cm³)		Particulate NO_3 (ng/cm³)		Gaseous HNO_3 (ng/cm³)		Gaseous SO_2 (ng/cm³)		Particulate SO_4 (ng/cm³)	
				trend	p-value	trend	p-value	trend	p-value	trend	p-value	trend	p-value
CAN407[1]	Canyonlands NP	1,809	Desert	--	0.130	--	0.372	--	0.186	-20.8	<0.001	-10.6	0.032
CNT169	Centennial	3,178	Forest	-1.5	0.048	--	0.557	--	0.978	-7.0	<0.001	-5.6	0.003
GLR468	Glacier NP	976	Forest	--	0.171	--	0.124	--	0.928	-11.8	0.003	-8.9	0.001
GTH16[1]	Gothic	2,926	Forest	-1.1	0.031	--	0.164	--	1.000	-3.0	0.003	-4.3	0.013
MEV405[1]	Mesa Verde NP	2,165	Forest	--	0.797	--	0.198	17.1	0.005	-46.9	0.000	--	0.318
PND165	Pinedale	2,388	Forest	-1.2	0.023	--	0.418	5.2	0.001	--	0.219	--	0.106
ROM406[1]	Rocky Mtn NP	2,743	Forest	--	0.124	--	0.873	--	0.472	-15.7	0.002	--	0.062
YEL408[1]	Yellowstone NP	2,400	Agriculture	--	0.273	--	0.492	--	0.635	--	0.182	--	0.360

[1]Trend tested for 1996 to 2008.

Table 7. Regional trends in annual mean minimum and maximum air temperature and precipitation amount for 12 groupings of National Resources Conservation Service Snow Telemetry (SNOTEL) stations in the Rocky Mountain region for 1990 to 2006.

[Mean elevation above North American Vertical Datum of 1988. Air temperature trends in degrees Celsius per decade; precipitation trends in inches per year; --, trend not statistically significant; dark blue shading indicates downward trend with p-value less than or equal to 0.01; dark orange shading indicates upward trend with p-value less than or equal to 0.01; light orange shading indicates upward trend with p-value greater than 0.01 and less than or equal to 0.05]

Mountain group	Stations per group	Median elevation (feet)	Annual mean minimum air temperature		Annual mean maximum air temperature		Annual mean precipitation	
			Trend	p-value	Trend	p-value	Trend	p-value
Salmon River Mountains	11	6,585	--	0.231	0.75	0.022	--	0.811
Bighorn Mountains	11	8,874	0.63	0.030	--	0.089	−0.43	0.007
Sawtooth Range	10	7,264	--	0.155	0.83	0.011	--	0.557
Wind River Range	14	8,694	--	0.090	--	0.517	--	0.194
Medicine Bow Mountains	11	9,112	0.74	0.010	1.02	0.004	--	0.676
Uinta Mountains	16	9,721	0.67	0.013	--	0.426	--	0.729
Front Range	14	9,744	0.74	0.039	0.63	0.018	--	0.514
Northern Colorado Ranges	10	9,576	0.68	0.008	--	0.259	--	0.789
Central Colorado Ranges	9	10,417	0.57	0.010	--	0.078	--	0.731
Sawatch/Elk Mountains	11	10,084	0.75	0.004	--	0.060	--	0.424
San Juan Mountains	19	10,418	0.58	0.007	0.78	0.032	--	0.221
Sangre de Cristo Range	8	10,369	0.71	0.002	0.70	0.049	--	0.052

Results of the RKT revealed statistically significant (p-value less than or equal to 0.050) upward trends in annual mean T_{min} for 9 of the 12 regional groupings (table 7; fig. 4). The magnitudes of trends in T_{min} were similar among groupings ranging from 0.57 to 0.75 °C per decade, indicating the amount of warming was fairly uniform. Spatial and temporal patterns in T_{min} are illustrated by plots of annual temperature anomalies for each group by year (fig. 10). The temperature anomaly is the annual mean minimum or maximum air temperature for each group minus the long-term average temperature for 1990–2006. The plots generally show a monotonic increase in T_{min} over the period of record punctuated by some colder years in 1993, 1997, and 2002. The warming trends appear to be more pronounced in Colorado than the northern groups in Wyoming and Idaho. Greater warming in Colorado compared to Wyoming and Idaho might reflect the higher elevation of the Colorado mountain groupings (table 7). Only 6 of the 12 groupings showed statistically significant trends in T_{max} and only one group had a p-value less than 0.01, indicating the trends in T_{max} were weaker than trends in T_{min}. Plots of temperature anomalies for T_{max} (fig. 11) show a strong increase in Colorado between 1993 and 2003, particularly in the San Juan Mountains and Sangre de Cristo Range. The mid-record rise in T_{max} was not as distinct among the northern mountain groupings. By season, the strongest increases in T_{min} were during the summer months (June, July, and August) with 9 of the 12 regions showing upward trends during summer with slopes ranging from 0.72 to 0.97 °C per decade. Only a few individual stations (12 of 144) and none of the regional groups

showed significant trends in T_{min} during spring, fall, or winter. Greater warming during summer could have implications for snowmelt timing (Clow, 2010) and reduced soil moisture in summer. Temperature trends reported in this study are consistent with the finding of Rangwala and Miller (2010) who reported a net warming of about 1 °C in the San Juan Mountains between 1895 and 2005, with most of the increase occurring after 1990. This warming in Colorado in recent decades is similar to patterns observed elsewhere in the United States (Rangwala and Miller, 2010); however, the magnitude of warming trends in these high-elevation areas such as the San Juan Mountains has been among the highest reported in the literature (Rangwala and Miller, 2010). These observed trends in air temperature appear to be consistent with those occurring globally (Intergovernmental Panel on Climate Change, 2007) and may indicate that human-induced warming could have a measureable effect on aquatic ecosystems in some high-elevation areas of the Rocky Mountains.

Trends in annual precipitation amounts at the SNOTEL stations were much weaker than those observed for air temperature (table 7). Of the 12 regional groupings, only the Bighorn Mountains showed a significant trend, which was downward. These results are consistent with the lack of trends in annual precipitation amount measured at the 23 NADP stations (table 3). Although precipitation amount did not show a monotonic change over the period of record, plots of annual precipitation anomalies (annual mean precipitation minus long-term average precipitation for 1990–2006) for the SNOTEL groups do reveal some short-term patterns. Precipitation amount was

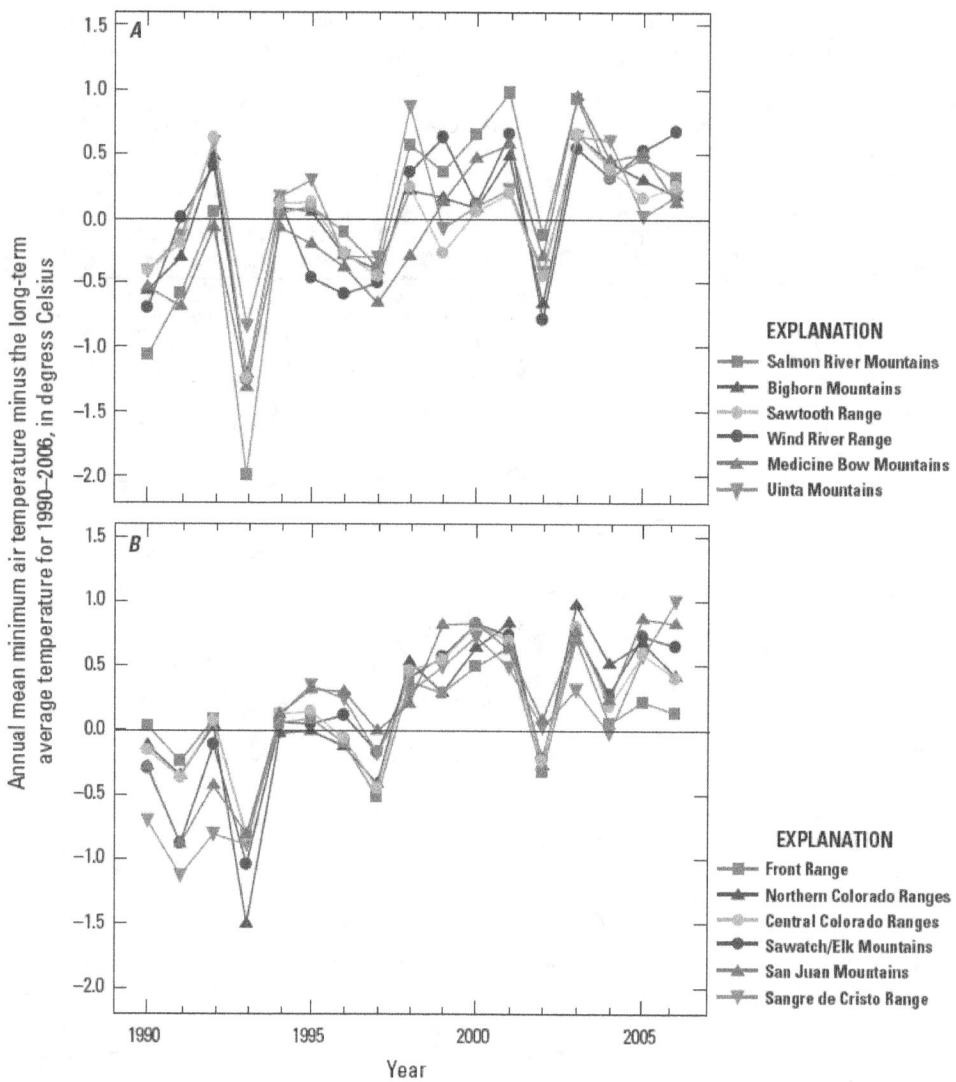

Figure 10. Anomalies in annual mean minimum air temperature at Snow Telemetry (SNOTEL) stations in 12 geographic groupings in (*A*) Wyoming, Idaho, and Utah and (*B*) Colorado for 1990 to 2006.

about average at the beginning and end of the period of record but showed a strong downward trend in the middle part of the record (fig. 12). This trend was caused by wetter than average years during 1995 to 1997 and drier years during 2001 to 2004.

Trends in Lake Chemistry in Selected Wilderness Areas

This section examines trends in the chemical composition of 64 high-elevation lakes representing 22 wilderness areas for the period 1993 through 2009. The 64 lakes were subdivided into 10 geographic groupings based on major mountain ranges (table 8 and fig. 1) to help examine spatial patterns in concentrations and trends. The study lakes were extremely

dilute as illustrated in figure 13 by the median concentrations of selected constituents in the 64 study lakes. Calcium plus magnesium were the dominant cations in lake water and ANC and sulfate were the dominant anions. Lakes in Sawatch/Elk Mountains and Sangre de Cristo Range in Colorado typically had higher calcium plus magnesium and ANC concentrations than other areas, perhaps due to presence of faster weathering mafic minerals such as hornblende or trace amounts of calcite in the bedrock (White and others, 2005). The most dilute lakes are in central Idaho, where the lake basins are underlain by granitic rock types, which tend to be slow weathering. Of the major constituents, sulfate showed the widest range of concentrations varying by over an order of magnitude. Lakes in central and southern Colorado tended to have the highest sulfate concentrations; a maximum concentration of 212 µeq/L was measured at Brooklyn Lake (site 47) in the Sawatch Range of

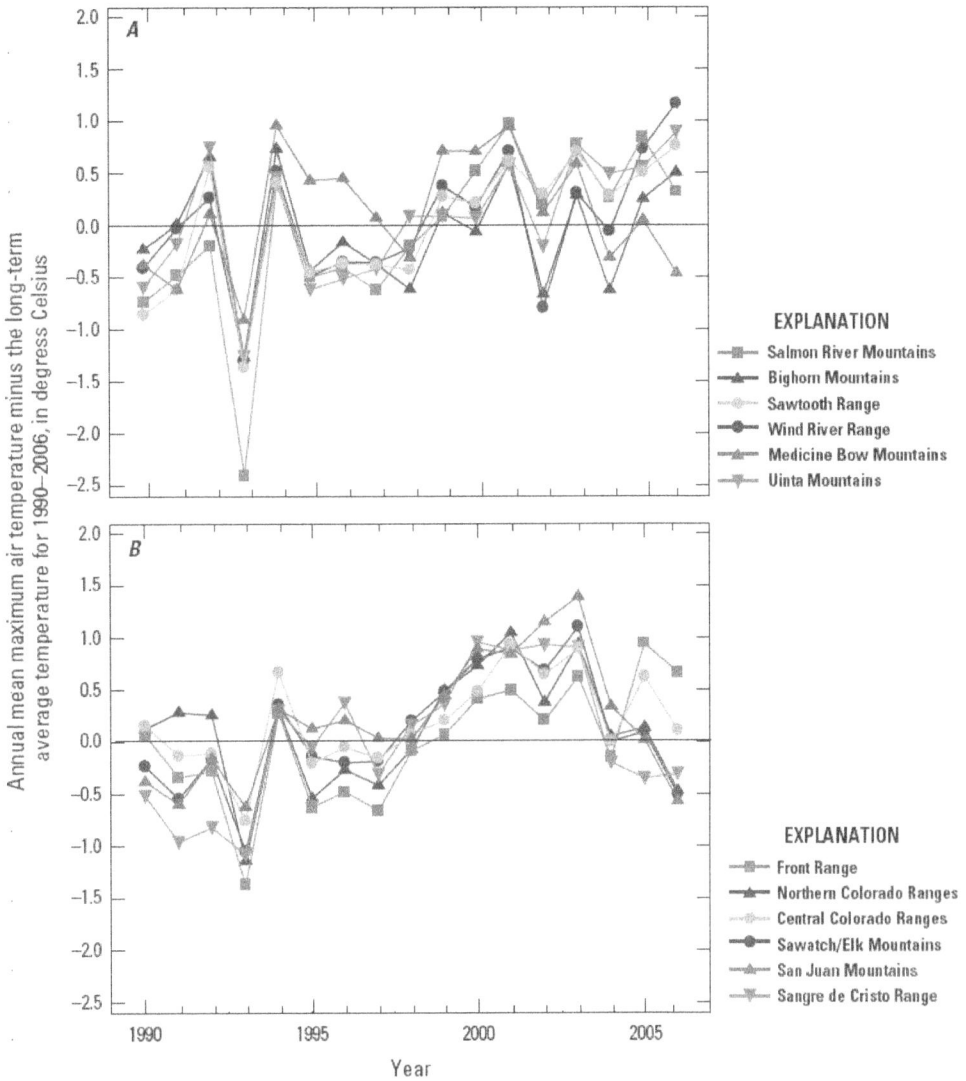

Figure 11. Anomalies in annual mean maximum air temperature at Snow Telemetry (SNOTEL) stations in 12 geographic groupings in (*A*) Wyoming, Idaho, and Utah and (*B*) Colorado for 1990 to 2006.

central Colorado (site number from table 1 and fig. 1). Many of these central Colorado lakes are in or adjacent to mineralized areas where the bedrock may contain deposits of pyrite, which release sulfate to surface water as they oxidize (Wanty and others, 2009). Chloride concentrations were very low and fairly uniform among the lakes, indicating atmospheric deposition is the dominant source of this constituent. Nitrate concentrations during the summer sampling period were near or below the analytical reporting limit (0.48 µeq/L) at most of the lakes likely due to active biological uptake; however, nitrate was detectable in several lakes notably Crater Lake (site 51) on the south end of the Sangre de Cristo Range and Upper Frozen Lake (station 9) in the Wind River Range. A few lakes

in the Front Range and Elk Mountains also had detectable nitrate concentrations during the summer sampling period.

Many statistically significant trends were detected in lake-water concentrations in the study lakes (table 8 and fig. 14). Most of the statistically significant trends were upward trends, and only sulfate showed a substantial number (11 sites) of downward trends. Specific conductance, pH, calcium, and sulfate showed statistically significant trends in about 70 percent of the lakes, and chloride and nitrate had trends in fewer than 20 percent of the lakes. Trend results for silica were only reported for the USGS stations because silica was not measured as part of the Forest Service monitoring program. For most of the lakes, the trend magnitude for the sum of base cations was very close to the sum of ANC plus

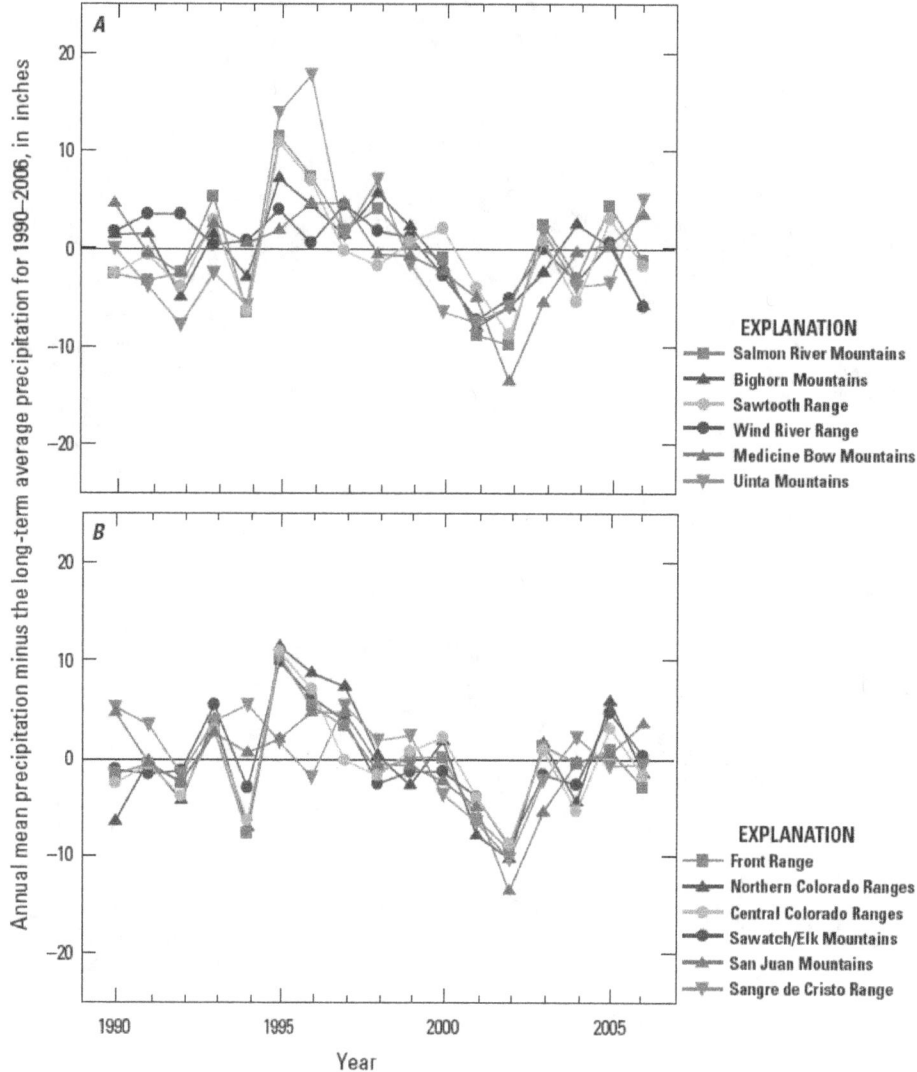

Figure 12.   Anomalies in annual mean precipitation amount at Snow Telemetry (SNOTEL) stations in 12 geographic groupings in (*A*) Wyoming, Idaho, and Utah and (*B*) Colorado for 1990 to 2006.

sulfate (r^2=0.92, slope=0.89), indicating that the trends reflect real changes in lake chemistry rather than artifacts of protocol or method changes. The median rate of change at lakes with significant trends was +2.5 microequivalents per liter per year (µeq/L/yr) for base cations, +1.8 µeq/L/yr for ANC, and +0.7 µeq/L/yr for sulfate. The largest change in lake chemistry was observed at Tabor Lake (site 42) in the Collegiate Peaks Wilderness (Sawatch/Elk Mountains) in central Colorado where calcium concentrations increased by nearly threefold and sulfate concentrations increased by more than ninefold during the 15-year period of record. The largest upward trends in ANC and base cations were detected for lakes in the Front Range and Sawatch/Elk Mountains. The largest increases in sulfate concentrations were detected for lakes in the Sawatch/

Elk Mountains and the Needle Mountains. Despite widespread declines in sulfate deposition, decreases in surface-water sulfate concentrations were mostly limited to lakes in the Zirkel/ Flat Tops Mountains.

Lake Chemical Response to Atmospheric Deposition

The response of surface-water chemistry to reductions in SO$_2$ emissions has been well documented in the Northeastern United States (Stoddard and others, 2003, Burns and others, 2006; Driscoll and others, 2003) and in Europe (Mosello and others, 2002), but few results have been reported for

Table 8. Trends in dissolved constituent concentrations for 64 high-elevation lakes in selected Class I wilderness areas for 1993 to 2009.

[Site no. from fig. 1; Begin date, begin date used in trend analysis; N, number of samples used in trend analysis; Spec cond, specific conductance in microsiemens per centimeter per year; pH in standard units per year; ANC, acid neutralizing capacity; trends for other constituents in microequivalents per liter per year; --, trend not statistically significant; x, insufficient data to compute trend; Mtns, Mountains; Mountains; dark blue shading indicates downward trend with p-value less than or equal to 0.01; light blue shading indicates downward trend with p-value greater than 0.01 and less than or equal to 0.05; dark orange shading indicates upward trend with p-value less than or equal to 0.01; light orange shading indicates upward trend with p-value greater than 0.01 and less than or equal to 0.05]

Site no.	Lake name	Mountain grouping	State	Begin date	N	Spec. cond.	pH	ANC	Cal-cium	Mag-nesium	Sod-ium	Potas-sium	Chlor-ide	Ni-trate	Sul-fate	Sili-ca
1	Ingeborg Lake	Sawtooth Range	Idaho	2002	8	--	0.03	1.75	--	--	--	--	--	x	--	x
2	Harbor Lake	Sawtooth Range	Idaho	1994	13	--	0.05	--	0.84	--	--	--	--	x	-0.06	x
3	No Name 4C1-048	Sawtooth Range	Idaho	1994	17	--	0.02	--	0.41	0.10	0.28	--	--	x	--	x
4	Lake 502A	Sawtooth Range	Idaho	2002	8	--	--	--	--	--	1.28	--	--	-0.06	--	x
5	No Name 4C1-049	Sawtooth Range	Idaho	1994	17	0.09	0.03	--	0.85	0.11	0.25	--	--	x	--	x
6	No Name 4C1-043	Sawtooth Range	Idaho	1994	13	--	--	--	--	--	--	--	--	x	--	x
7	Florence Lake	Bighorn Mountains	Wyo.	1994	45	0.27	0.05	--	1.54	0.36	0.46	0.15	--	--	0.61	x
8	Emerald Lake	Bighorn Mountains	Wyo.	1994	42	0.16	0.05	--	0.85	0.18	--	0.13	--	x	0.19	x
9	Upper Frozen Lake	Wind River Range	Wyo.	1997	11	--	0.04	--	1.01	0.33	0.17	--	--	x	0.25	x
10	Ross Lake	Wind River Range	Wyo.	1993	49	0.10	0.02	--	--	--	0.20	0.09	--	x	--	x
11	Lower Saddlebag Lake	Wind River Range	Wyo.	1993	51	0.21	0.03	0.86	0.92	0.23	0.33	0.12	--	--	0.18	x
12	Hobbs Lake	Wind River Range	Wyo.	1993	54	0.10	0.02	--	--	--	0.24	--	--	x	--	x
13	Deep Lake	Wind River Range	Wyo.	1995	45	0.20	0.03	--	0.76	0.14	0.40	0.11	--	x	0.34	x
14	Black Joe Lake	Wind River Range	Wyo.	1993	57	0.28	0.03	0.90	1.28	0.23	0.46	0.16	0.11	--	0.77	x
15	Dean Lake	Uinta Mountains	Utah	2001	8	--	0.03	2.22	--	--	--	--	--	x	--	x
16	Walkup Lake	Uinta Mountains	Utah	2002	8	--	--	--	--	--	--	--	--	--	--	x
17	Fish Lake	Uinta Mountains	Utah	2002	8	--	--	--	--	--	--	--	--	x	--	x
18	Upper Ned Wilson Lake	Zirkel/Flat Tops	Colo.	1993	82	0.12	--	1.35	0.99	0.28	0.07	0.04	0.03	x	-0.13	0.17
19	Lower NWL Packtrail Pothole	Zirkel/Flat Tops	Colo.	1993	87	--	--	0.79	0.61	0.09	--	--	--	x	-0.22	x
20	Ned Wilson Lake	Zirkel/Flat Tops	Colo.	1993	84	0.10	--	1.24	0.81	0.24	0.10	0.08	0.02	x	-0.16	x
21	Upper NWL Packtrail Pothole	Zirkel/Flat Tops	Colo.	1993	85	0.07	-0.01	1.14	0.77	0.30	--	0.04	--	--	-0.16	x
22	Seven Lakes	Zirkel/Flat Tops	Colo.	1993	47	--	--	0.66	0.33	0.11	--	--	0.04	x	-0.18	x
23	Summit Lake	Zirkel/Flat Tops	Colo.	1993	57	0.16	--	1.90	1.26	0.30	0.19	0.06	0.07	x	-0.30	0.66
24	Lake Elbert	Zirkel/Flat Tops	Colo.	1993	49	--	--	--	--	--	--	--	--	x	-0.31	0.40
25	No Name 4E1-055	Front Range	Colo.	1996	25	0.19	0.06	1.52	1.09	0.28	0.28	--	--	x	--	x
26	Blue Lake	Front Range	Colo.	1996	39	0.41	0.04	1.36	2.52	0.44	0.82	0.10	--	--	1.69	x
27	Rawah Lake #4	Front Range	Colo.	1996	26	0.34	0.06	2.27	1.86	0.22	0.53	0.26	0.06	x	0.33	x
28	King Lake	Front Range	Colo.	1996	28	0.39	0.05	2.04	2.14	0.77	0.79	0.12	--	x	0.80	x
29	Crater Lake	Front Range	Colo.	1996	27	0.32	0.06	1.41	2.84	0.26	0.35	0.07	--	x	0.56	x

Table 8. Trends in dissolved constituent concentrations for 64 high-elevation lakes in selected Class I wilderness areas for 1993 to 2009.—Continued

[Site no. from fig. 1; Begin date, begin date used in trend analysis; N, number of samples used in trend analysis; Spec cond, specific conductance in microsiemens per centimeter per year, pH in standard units per year; ANC, acid neutralizing capacity; trends for other constituents in microequivalents per liter per year; --, trend not statistically significant; x, insufficient data to compute trend; Mtns, Mountains; dark blue shading indicates downward trend with p-value less than or equal to 0.01; light blue shading indicates downward trend with p-value greater than 0.01 and less than or equal to 0.05; dark orange shading indicates upward trend with p-value less than or equal to 0.01; light orange shading indicates upward trend with p-value greater than 0.01 and less than or equal to 0.05]

Site no.	Lake name	Mountain grouping	State	Begin date	N	Spec. cond.	pH	ANC	Cal-cium	Mag-nesium	Sod-ium	Potas-sium	Chlor-ide	Ni-trate	Sul-fate	Sili-ca
30	Island Lake	Front Range	Colo.	1996	26	0.52	0.07	3.11	3.58	0.59	0.64	0.31	--	--	0.43	x
31	Upper Middle Beartrack Lake	Front Range	Colo.	1994	40	--	0.02	--	--	--	--	0.32	--	--	--	x
32	Upper Lake	Front Range	Colo.	1995	29	0.37	0.05	--	--	--	0.52	--	--	--	1.05	x
33	Frozen Lake	Front Range	Colo.	1994	43	0.56	0.04	1.55	3.45	0.69	0.65	0.18	0.08	0.18	1.40	x
34	Abyss Lake	Front Range	Colo.	1994	45	0.74	0.04	1.27	4.28	0.62	1.30	0.24	0.12	0.29	2.30	x
35	Kelly Lake	Front Range	Colo.	1995	28	0.59	0.07	2.36	2.53	0.62	0.63	0.24	--	x	1.00	x
36	Deep Creek Lake	Sawatch/Elk Mountains	Colo.	1995	28	0.10	0.04	--	--	0.07	0.16	--	--	x	--	x
37	Blodgett Lake	Sawatch/Elk Mountains	Colo.	1996	42	0.26	0.05	1.94	1.91	0.54	0.41	0.12	0.04	--	0.37	x
38	Moon Lake (Upper)	Sawatch/Elk Mountains	Colo.	1993	51	0.33	0.06	2.67	2.31	0.26	0.38	0.10	--	--	--	x
39	Booth Lake	Sawatch/Elk Mountains	Colo.	1995	45	0.20	0.05	1.19	0.88	0.48	0.25	0.09	--	--	-0.14	x
40	South Golden Lake	Sawatch/Elk Mountains	Colo.	1995	23	0.52	0.07	1.83	2.41	0.33	--	--	--	--	0.46	x
41	Upper Turquoise Lake	Sawatch/Elk Mountains	Colo.	1996	41	0.56	0.05	1.77	3.30	0.56	0.87	0.14	--	--	1.55	x
42	Tabor Lake	Sawatch/Elk Mountains	Colo.	1993	51	1.03	0.06	3.01	6.79	0.86	0.84	0.10	--	--	4.35	x
43	Upper West Tennessee Lake	Sawatch/Elk Mountains	Colo.	1996	44	0.84	0.06	3.51	4.68	1.41	0.75	--	--	x	2.71	x
44	Upper Willow Lake	Sawatch/Elk Mountains	Colo.	1994	45	0.56	0.10	3.37	4.35	1.23	0.53	0.18	0.07	--	0.47	x
45	Capitol Lake	Sawatch/Elk Mountains	Colo.	1993	50	0.64	0.05	--	3.04	0.56	0.56	0.10	0.11	--	1.21	x
46	Avalanche Lake	Sawatch/Elk Mountains	Colo.	1993	49	0.57	0.07	3.17	3.91	0.20	0.54	0.11	--	--	0.83	x
47	Brooklyn Lake	Sawatch/Elk Mountains	Colo.	1993	50	2.29	0.05	4.11	15.25	2.48	0.80	0.12	--	--	13.25	x
48	Upper Stout Lake	Sangre de Cristo Range	Colo.	1996	39	0.34	0.05	--	1.84	0.39	--	0.20	--	--	0.76	x
49	Lower Stout Lake	Sangre de Cristo Range	Colo.	1996	41	0.55	0.05	--	1.78	0.42	0.25	0.23	--	0.15	1.43	x
50	Upper Little Sand Creek Lake	Sangre de Cristo Range	Colo.	1995	37	--	0.10	0.16	--	--	--	--	--	--	--	x
51	Crater Lake, Sangre De Cristo	Sangre de Cristo Range	Colo.	1996	23	--	0.06	--	--	--	--	0.15	--	--	2.47	x
52	White Dome Lake	Needle Mountains	Colo.	1993	35	0.24	--	--	1.39	0.46	--	--	--	--	1.01	x
53	Little Eldorado Lake	Needle Mountains	Colo.	1993	34	0.34	--	--	1.55	0.29	--	--	--	--	2.10	x
54	Upper Grizzly Lake	Needle Mountains	Colo.	1993	28	--	--	0.16	--	0.31	0.19	--	0.08	--	0.97	x
55	Upper Sunlight Lake	Needle Mountains	Colo.	1993	32	0.76	0.01	1.14	4.62	1.16	0.36	0.09	--	--	4.56	0.16
56	Big Eldorado Lake	Needle Mountains	Colo.	1993	36	0.64	--	--	2.94	2.34	--	0.05	0.05	--	4.82	0.29
57	Lower Sunlight Lake	Needle Mountains	Colo.	1993	32	0.55	--	1.88	4.33	0.59	0.31	0.07	--	--	2.57	x
58	Lake south of Ute Lake	Sawatch/Elk Mtns	Colo.	1993	20	-0.12	--	--	-0.44	--	--	--	--	x	-0.65	x

Trends in Lake Chemistry in Selected Wilderness Areas   31

Table 8. Trends in dissolved constituent concentrations for 64 high-elevation lakes in selected Class I wilderness areas for 1993 to 2009.—Continued

[Site no. from fig. 1; Begin date, begin date used in trend analysis; N, number of samples used in trend analysis; Spec cond, specific conductance in microsiemens per centimeter per year; pH in standard units per year; ANC, acid neutralizing capacity; trends for other constituents in microequivalents per liter per year. --, trend not statistically significant; x, insufficient data to compute trend; Mtns, Mountains; dark blue shading indicates downward trend with p-value less than or equal to 0.01; dark orange shading indicates upward trend with p-value less than or equal to 0.01; light orange shading indicates upward trend with p-value greater than 0.01 and less than or equal to 0.05]

Site no.	Lake name	Mountain grouping	State	Begin date	N	Spec. cond.	pH	ANC	Cal-cium	Mag-nesium	Sod-ium	Potas-sium	Chlor-ide	Ni-trate	Sul-fate	Sili-ca
59	Lake south of Blue Lakes	Sawatch/Elk Mtns	Colo.	1993	31	0.19	0.04	1.52	1.45	0.28	0.40	0.38	--	X	--	X
60	Small Pond above Trout Lake	Sawatch/Elk Mtns	Colo.	1993	28	--	--	--	--	--	--	--	--	--	-0.56	X
61	Middle Ute Lake	Sawatch/Elk Mtns	Colo.	1993	23	--	0.03	--	--	--	--	--	--	X	--	X
62	Glacier Lake	Sawatch/Elk Mtns	Colo.	1993	30	0.12	0.03	--	0.65	--	--	0.14	0.06	X	--	X
63	Lake above U-Shaped Lake	Sawatch/Elk Mtns	Colo.	1994	22	0.51	0.05	2.36	--	--	1.12	0.17	0.09	0.26	--	X
64	U-Shaped Lake	Sawatch/Elk Mtns	Colo.	1994	20	0.44	0.07	--	1.67	--	0.96	--	--	--	--	X

acid-sensitive lakes and streams in the Western United States. The analysis of precipitation chemistry in the Rocky Mountain region clearly shows that sulfate (and hydrogen ion) concentrations in deposition have decreased in high-elevation areas over the past two decades as a result of emissions reductions. Despite widespread declines in deposition, the response of high-elevation lakes has been quite variable; about one-third of the lakes, showed trends in lake-water sulfate concentrations that were opposite to those in deposition. However; there were significant declines in lake-water sulfate concentrations in a few lakes, notably those in the Zirkel/Flat Tops Mountains in northwestern Colorado (fig. 14). In these areas, significant downward trends were detected in all seven lakes sampled, and the rate of decline ranged from –0.13 to –0.31 µeq/L/yr. The magnitude of trends was fairly uniform and compared well with the mean decrease of –0.24 µeq/L/yr for sulfate in precipitation, indicating lake chemistry in these areas appears to be responding to decreased SO_2 emissions and atmospheric-sulfate deposition. The link between lake chemistry and deposition is further supported by sulfur isotopic data reported by Mast and others (2011) for the USGS lakes (table 1). The results, which are summarized in figure 15, show good agreement between isotopic values in precipitation and surface water confirming that deposition is the dominant source of lake-water sulfate in the Zirkel/Flat Tops Mountains. In contrast, the isotopic data for lakes in the Needle Mountains indicate dissolved sulfate was derived primarily from pyrite (Mast and others, 2011). Given the weathering sources can be a substantial source of lake-water sulfate, it is not surprising that trends in atmospheric sulfate deposition had a minimal effect on lake chemistry throughout the region. Low sulfate concentrations in the Sawtooth Range and San Juan/La Garita Mountains (fig. 13) indicate that sulfate in these lakes primarily is derived from atmospheric deposition; however, few of these lakes showed sulfate trends. Lack of trends might reflect a shorter period of record and paucity of data at some lakes, particularly sites in Idaho (table 8).

More detailed analysis of lakes showing downward sulfate trends reveals that declines in sulfate at Summit Lake (site 23) and Lake Elbert (site 24) in the Mount Zirkel Wilderness are almost twice that of trends for lakes in the Flat Tops Wilderness (sites 18, 20) (table 8). Somewhat larger decreases might be expected at these two lakes in the Mount Zirkel Wilderness because they are directly downwind from the Craig and Hayden coal-fired powerplants (fig. 3). SO_2 emissions have decreased by more than 80 percent at the two plants since 2000 following installation of gas and particulate control systems (Mast and others, 2005). If sulfate trends are computed for the post-control period of 2000 to 2009 (fig. 16), Summit Lake (site 23), the closest site to the powerplants, shows a larger decrease in sulfate (–0.57 µeq/L/yr) compared to Ned Wilson Lake (site 20), which is farther from the source and not downwind (-0.07 µeq/L/y). The greater trend at Summit Lake may indicate surface-water chemistry is responding to emission declines at the local powerplants as well as from regional sources. These results are consistent with deposition

data, which also show larger decreases in sulfate at NADP stations and RMSN sites downwind from the powerplants; in particular, Dry Lake, Buffalo Pass, and Rabbit Ears Pass (tables 3 and 5).

Although wet deposition of nitrogen species exceeds that of sulfate at all the NADP stations, nitrate concentrations in most lakes were at or near the reporting limit (0.48 µeq/L), indicating terrestrial and aquatic biota uptake of atmospherically deposited nitrogen at least during the growing season when lake sampling occurred. Abyss Lake (site 34), Crater Lake (site 51), Lake above U-Shaped Lake (site 63), and Upper Frozen Lake (site 9) consistently had the highest nitrate concentrations, as much as 10 µeq/L. Nitrate also was commonly above the reporting limit at lakes in the Needle and in the Sawatch Mountains. Baron and others (2010) proposed a reference condition of 0.1 mg/L nitrate (or 1.6 µeq/L) for lakes in Rocky Mountain National Park and suggested that growing season concentrations above this level may indicate that watersheds have reached nitrogen saturation. Increased lake nitrate concentrations may stimulate growth of nitrogen-rich algal assemblages, which are poor food quality for zooplankton and may eventually alter nutritional dynamics up the food chain to fish (Elser and others, 2009). Elevated nitrate has been reported at high-elevation lakes and streams on the east side of the Front Range where surface-water concentrations typically exceed 15 µeq/L during the summer growing season (Williams and others, 1996; Campbell and others, 2000). These watersheds are thought to be at an advanced stage of nitrogen saturation because of prolonged atmospheric nitrogen loading from source areas in eastern Colorado (Baron and others, 2000; Burns, 2004; Bowman and others, 2006). Abyss (site 34) and Crater (site 51) Lakes are located east of the Continental Divide and likely are subject to high levels of nitrogen deposition, but the other lakes are more distant from nitrogen emission sources. Elevation also may influence the nitrate levels of these lakes, which are all above 12,200 feet except for Upper Frozen Lake (site 9). Higher elevation watersheds typically have less capacity to retain nitrogen because of sparse soils and steep slopes (Sueker and others, 2001), lower in-lake productivity, and a shorter growing season (Sickman and others, 2002). The reason for the elevated nitrate in Upper Frozen Lake (site 9) is not known, although it is the highest of the study lakes sampled in the Wind River Range.

Of the 39 lakes that had sufficient nitrate data to calculate temporal trends, four showed upward trends in concentration and one showed a small downward trend (table 8). The strongest upward trends (table 8) were detected at Abyss (site 34), Frozen (site 33), and Lower Stout (site 49) Lakes, which are located east of the Continental Divide in Colorado (fig. 1). Concentrations at all three lakes increased until the mid-2000s then decreased slightly toward the end of the record (fig. 17). One explanation is that nitrate concentration trends in the lakes might be caused by increases in atmospheric nitrogen deposition, because most of the NADP stations east of the Continental Divide showed increases in ammonium concentrations (table 3). Another possibility is that

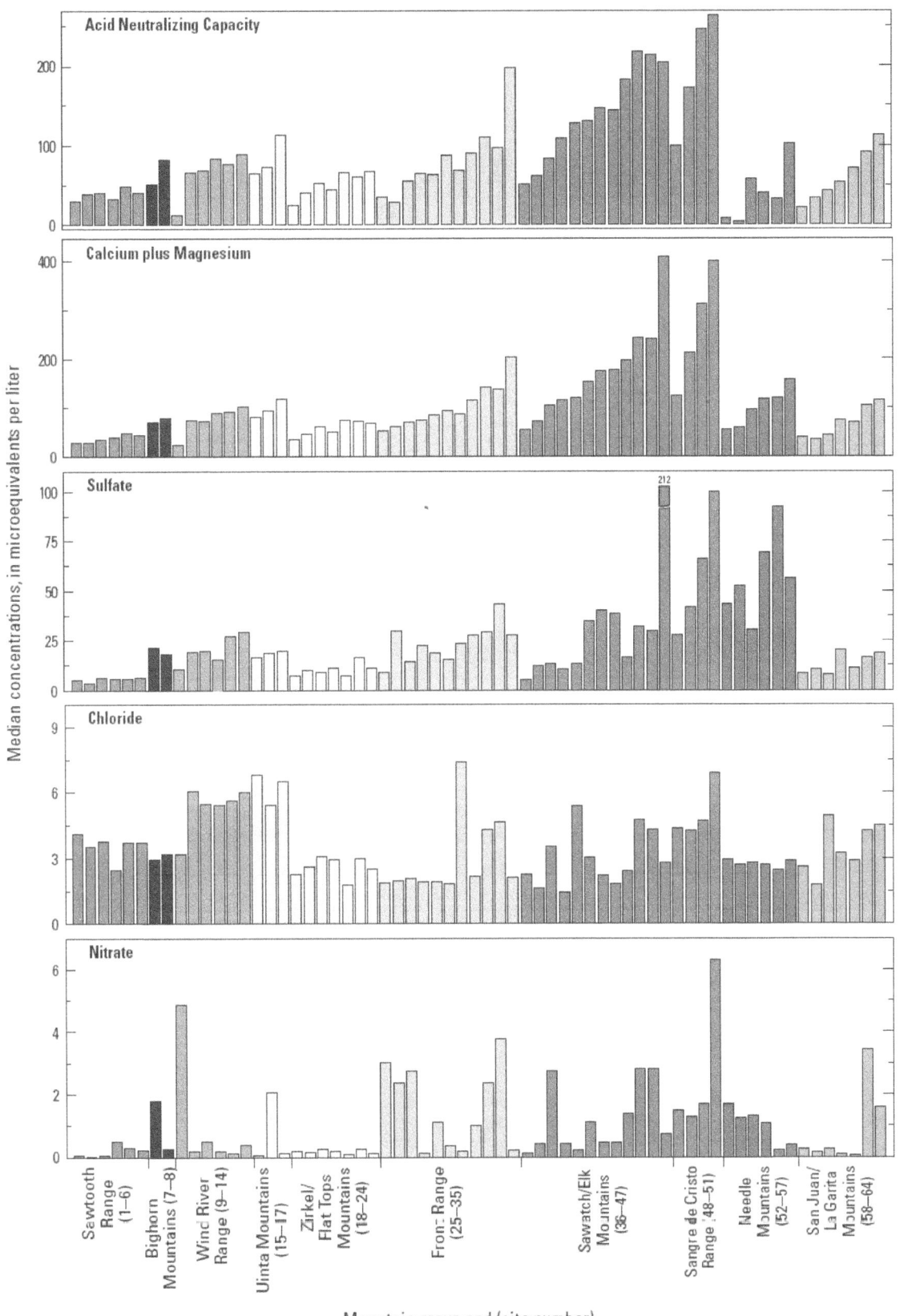

Figure 13. Median concentrations of acid neutralizing capacity, calcium plus magnesium, sulfate, chloride, and nitrate in the 64 study lakes grouped by major mountain range for 1993 to 2009.

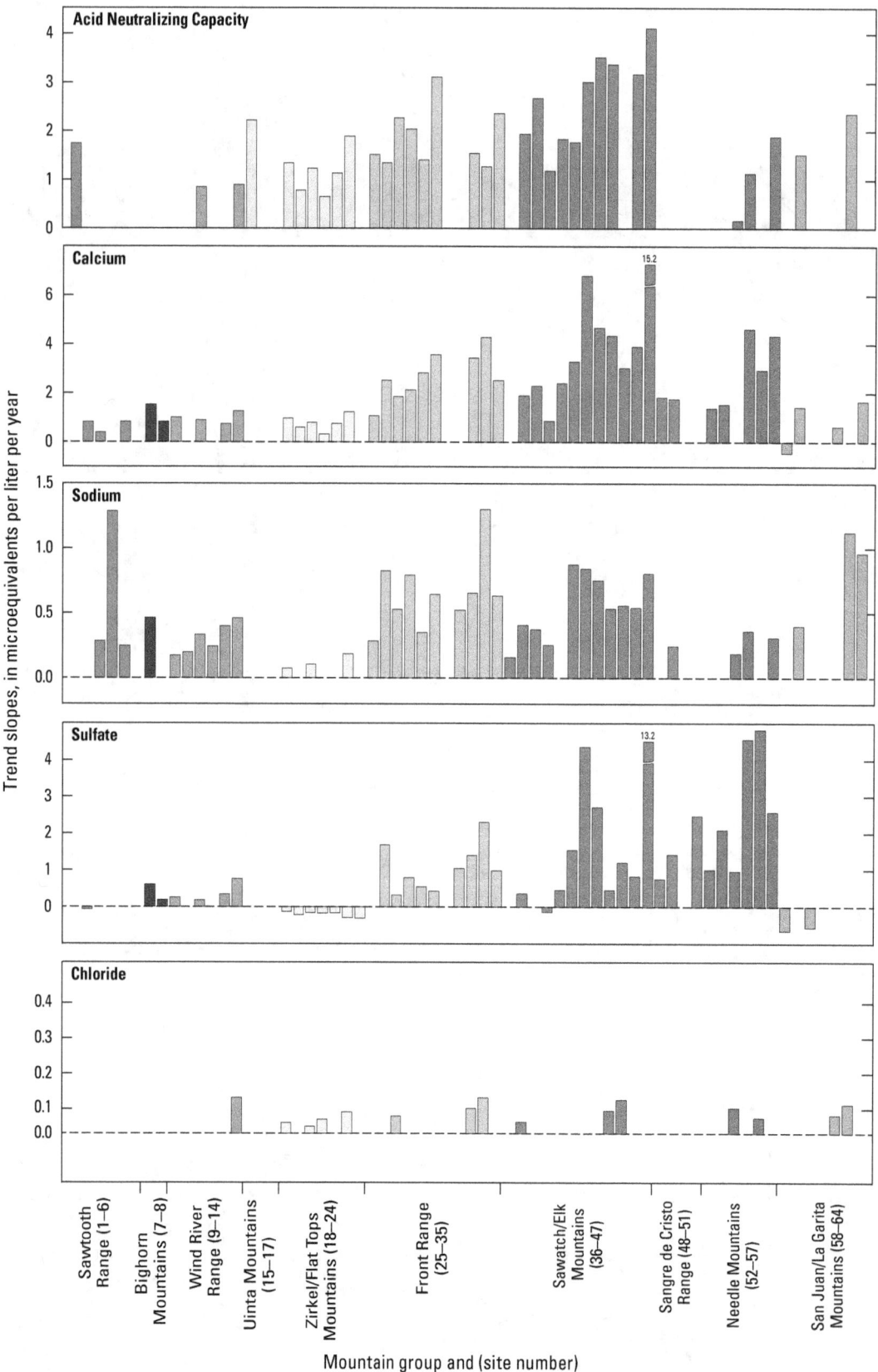

Figure 14.   Trends in concentration of selected dissolved constituents in the 64 study lakes grouped by major mountain range for 1993 to 2009.

the lake watersheds may be reaching an early stage of nitrogen saturation, where the input of nitrogen is not balanced by biotic uptake, and nitrate is starting to leach to surface waters, similar to what has been reported along the eastern flanks of the Front Range (Burns, 2004). Considering the variable nature of watersheds to assimilate nitrogen and susceptibility of nitrate to watershed disturbance and climate variation (Driscoll and others, 2003; Watmough and others, 2004), it is difficult to establish a link between lake-nitrate trends and atmospheric deposition with the relatively sparse data set available for these lakes and the effect of biota on nitrogen cycling.

Lake Chemical Response to Climate

The trend analysis revealed substantial increases in lake-water sulfate concentrations, particularly at lakes in the Front Range, Sawatch/Elk Mountains, Sangre de Cristo Range, and Needle Mountains in Colorado (fig. 18). The trends in sulfate were quite striking in some lakes. For example, at Tabor Lake (site 42) in the Sawatch/Elk Mountains, sulfate increased from a minimum of around 15 µeq/L in the mid-1990s to a peak of 140 µeq/L in 2009 (fig. 19A), and at Upper Sunlight Lake (statopmion 55) in the Needle Mountains, sulfate increased from around 50 µeq/L in the early 1990's to a peak of 180 µeq/L in 2003 (fig. 19B). In some lakes, particularly those in the Front Range and Sawatch/Elk Mountains, substantial increases in ANC were equal to or exceeded those in sulfate (fig. 18). Sulfur isotopic results for lakes in the Needle Mountains (fig. 15) clearly show that dissolved sulfate is mainly derived from weathering of pyrite. Although isotopic

data are not available for the other study lakes, many wilderness areas in Colorado are within or adjacent to the Colorado Mineral Belt (fig. 1), which is a northeast-trending zone of hydrothermal alteration and mineralization in central Colorado (Wilson and Sims, 2003). The mineral belt is an area with high background concentrations of sulfate and dissolved metals that are mobilized by weathering of pyrite and other sulfide minerals in altered and mineralized rocks (Wanty and others, 2009). Some studies have suggested sulfate minerals such as gypsum as the source of calcium and sulfate to alpine lakes and streams (Sommaruga-Wögrath and others, 1997); however, the isotopic evidence indicates this is not a plausible source, at least in the Needle Mountains where gypsum has a much heavier (+15 to +18 per mil) sulfur isotopic ratio (Mast and others, 2011). Increases in lake-water sulfate and ANC predominantly were balanced by increases in calcium and to a lesser extent magnesium (fig. 18). Calcium most likely comes from weathering of calcite, which occurs within mineralized veins and is disseminated within the silicate bedrock types that underlie most of the lake basins (White and others, 2005). Silicate minerals such as chlorite, epidote, and hornblende are the most likely sources of magnesium. A similar geochemical model was used to explain the chemical composition of a rock glacier outflow in the Colorado Front Range (Williams and others, 2006). Williams and others (2006) proposed that dissolution of pyrite, epidote, chlorite, and calcite best explained the substantial increases in sulfate, calcium, and magnesium concentrations observed at the outflow following a period of drought.

Upward trends in base cations, ANC, and sulfate could partly be explained by below-average precipitation and runoff, which might result in less dilution of weathering-derived

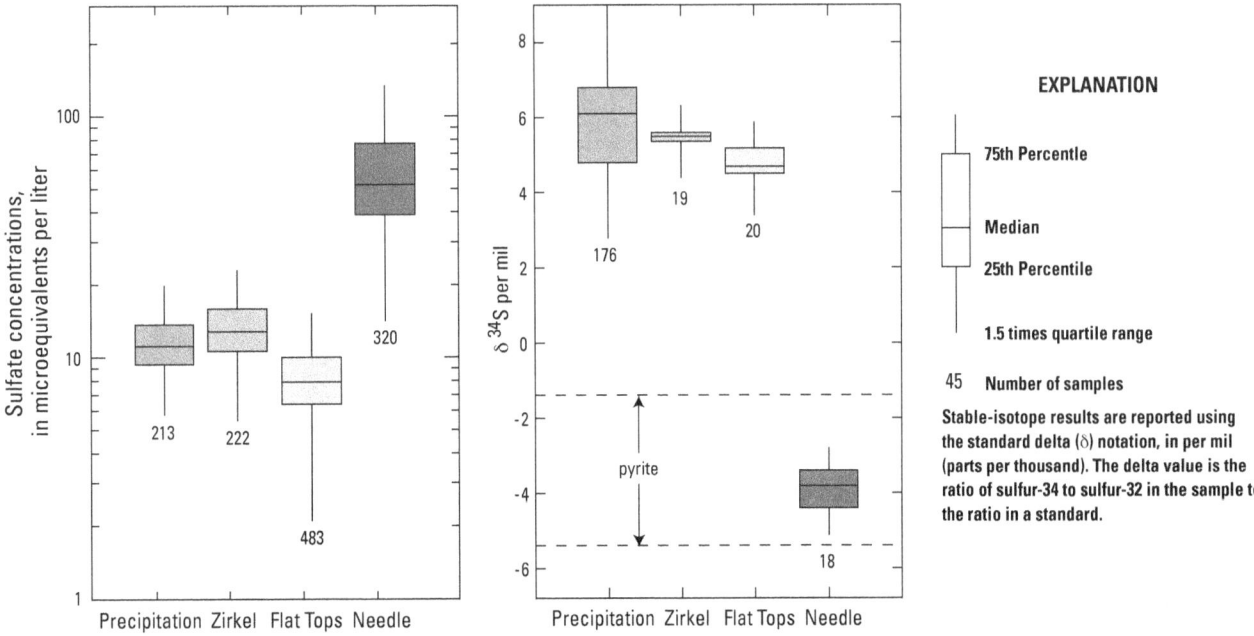

Figure 15. Range of sulfate concentrations and sulfur isotopic ratios in precipitation (rain and snow) and lake-water samples from the Zirkel, Flat Tops, and Needle Mountains in Colorado.

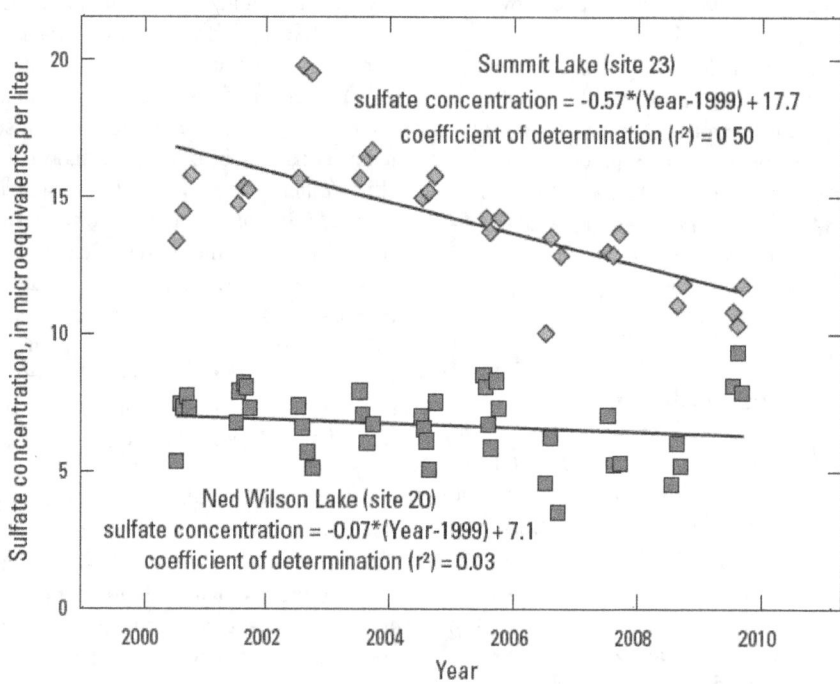

Figure 16. Downward trends in sulfate concentrations at Summit Lake in the Mount Zirkel Wilderness and Ned Wilson Lake in the Flat Tops Wilderness for 2000 to 2009.

solutes and a greater proportion of base-flow (groundwater) contributions to surface-water bodies. As noted in the Trends in Climate Variables in the Rocky Mountain Region section, there were few trends in annual precipitation at SNOTEL stations over the period 1990 to 2006; however, there was a downward trend in the middle part of the record due to wetter than average years during the mid-1990s and drier years during the early 2000s (fig. 12). Trends computed for each SNOTEL geographic group indicate average annual precipitation declined between 34 to 44 percent over the period 1995 to 2002. Time-series plots of lake-water concentrations reveal that trends at some lakes may partly be explained by declining precipitation, whereas the effect at other lakes is not as clear. At Capitol Lake (site 45) in the Sawatch/Elk Mountains (fig. 19C), for example, chloride concentrations showed an increase between 1996 and 2004 that largely mirrored the increase in lake sulfate. Assuming chloride is conservative and watershed sources are minimal, the similarity in patterns indicates trends at some lakes may simply reflect an increasing base-flow component in lake water. By contrast, the chemical response at Tabor Lake (site 42) in the Collegiate Peaks (fig. 1) was strikingly different; chloride concentrations showed little change over the period of decreasing precipitation whereas sulfate concentrations increased substantially following the period of declining precipitation (fig. 19A). The different patterns were unexpected considering the proximity of the lakes and suggest that relative inputs from different groundwater sources changed during the drought or alternatively that

precipitation/runoff may not be the only factor driving the long-term changes in lake chemistry. The influence of precipitation also was evident on shorter time scales. Following a severe regional drought in 2002 (Doesken and Pielke, 2003), a sudden increase in sulfate was observed at some of the lakes that persisted for a few years despite subsequent increases in precipitation (fig. 19C). Pulses of sulfate-rich water following drought have been documented in headwater streams in North America; however, these pulses mainly occurred in wetland-dominated catchments because of drought-induced reoxidation of reduced sulfur in organic rich soils (Laudon and others, 2004; Eimers and others, 2007).

Some of the study lakes also showed increases in nitrate concentrations in years following the 2002 drought. Reduced snowcover during periods of drought has been reported to increase catchment nitrogen leaching because of colder soil temperatures in winter and reduced microbial activity (De Wit and others, 2008). This mechanism might help explain the upward nitrate trends observed at a few of the study lakes (fig. 17) because nitrate increases were coincident with the period of declining precipitation (and snowpack). These patterns in lake-water nitrate may indicate that changes in climate, such as increased frequency of drought, could exacerbate the effects of nitrogen deposition on high-elevation lakes (Rogora and others, 2007). Many of these watersheds may be near the tipping point or critical load for nitrogen and continued monitoring will be important for detecting any changes in water quality that might negatively affect aquatic biota.

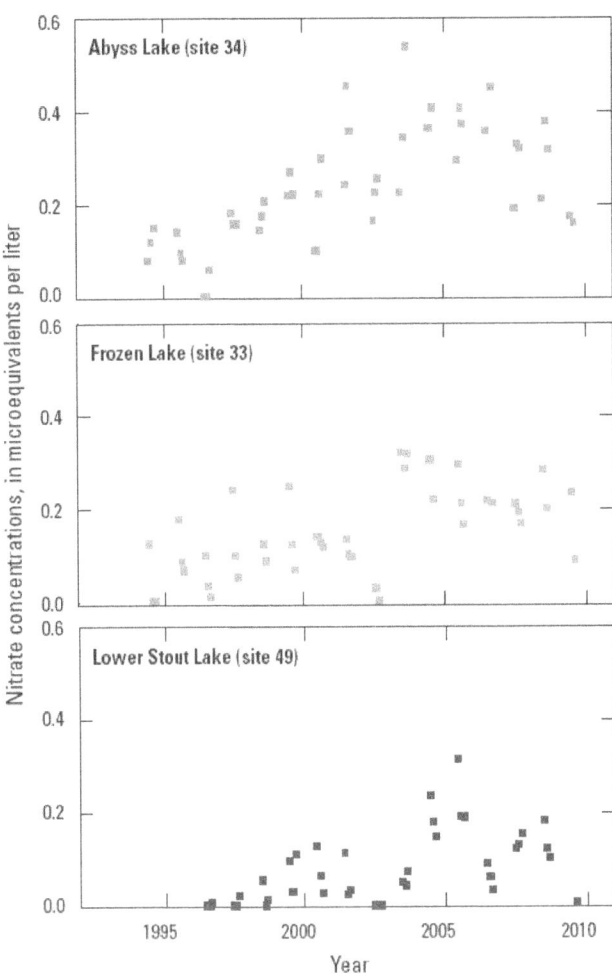

Figure 17. Trends in nitrate concentrations in three high-elevation lakes east of the Continental Divide for 1993 to 2009.

Although hydrologic conditions may partly explain the long-term changes in lake chemistry, it seems plausible that trends in air temperature also may be a factor. Similar increases in solute concentrations have been observed for numerous alpine lakes in Europe (Sommaruga-Wögrath and others, 1997; Tait and Thaler, 2000; Mosello and others, 2002; Rogora and others, 2003) and have been attributed to enhanced weathering rates and increased biological activity caused by increasing air temperatures (Sommaruga-Wögrath and others, 1997). The increase in annual air temperature in the Alps of +0.57 °C per decade for 1974 to 2004 (Rebetez and Reinhard, 2007) is similar to the Rocky Mountain region where trends averaged +0.68 °C per decade for 1990 to 2006 (Clow, 2010). Seasonal analyses showed that the greatest temperature increase in the Alps occurred during spring and summer (Rebetez and Reinhard, 2007), which is similar to the pattern in the Rocky Mountains where warming appeared to be strongest during the summer months (Clow, 2010). Sommaruga-Wögrath and others (1997) suggest one effect

of higher air temperatures, particularly during summer, is a shorter period of snow and ice cover, which increases exposure of rocks and soils and enhances weathering rates. Mast and others (2011) used data from SNOTEL stations in southwestern Colorado to estimate snow-cover duration based on the number of days per year with snow on the sensor pillow. The majority of stations showed no change over the period of record indicating that changes in snow cover duration probably has not been a major factor in the chemical changes observed for the study lakes.

Several recent studies have suggested the effect of climate warming on water chemistry in alpine areas is related to enhanced melting of ice features such as permafrost, rock glaciers, and glaciers (Williams and others, 2006; Thies and others, 2007; Hill, 2008; Baron and others, 2009). Thies and others (2007) reported as much as a 26-fold increase in sulfate and unexpectedly high concentrations of nickel and zinc during the past 20 years in alpine lakes in the Austrian Alps. Baron and others (2009) reported increasing calcium and sulfate concentrations since 2000 in streams draining an alpine watershed on the east side of the Colorado Front Range. Both these studies attribute chemical trends to greater contributions of rock-glacier meltwater, which can be highly enriched in dissolved solids because of high rates of chemical and physical weathering in periglacial environments (Brown, 2002; Williams and others, 2006). Baron and others (2009) also reported increases in stream nitrate, which were attributed to flushing of nitrogen from microbially active sediments exposed by the melting ice (Baron and others, 2009). Enhanced melting of permanent ice is plausible in Colorado given that recent air temperature trends have increased the elevation at which permafrost and permanent snow and ice can persist (Clow and others, 2003). Two recent studies in the Front Range have documented increases in late-season streamflow that have been attributed to melting glaciers and subsurface ice in rock glaciers and permafrost (Hill, 2008; Baron and others, 2009). The effect of melting permafrost on the chemistry of the study lakes is difficult to assess due to the unknown extent of permafrost as well as a lack of detailed hydrologic data. Although only a few of the lake basins contain permanent snowfields or rock glaciers, most of them contain numerous talus slopes and other periglacial features that could contain embedded ice or discontinuous permafrost (Millar and Westfall, 2008). Regional joint and fracture systems in the bedrock also might provide some storage for permanent ice. Because such fracture systems can be mineralized, melting of ice could enhance weathering of pyrite and other vein-filling minerals, resulting in increased solute transport to lakes. The magnitude of this input is unknown; however, a recent groundwater study of a mineralized alpine catchment in central Colorado found that simple topography rather than faults and lithology controlled the occurrence and flow of shallow groundwater (Manning and others, 2008), indicating that contributions from fracture flow would likely be small.

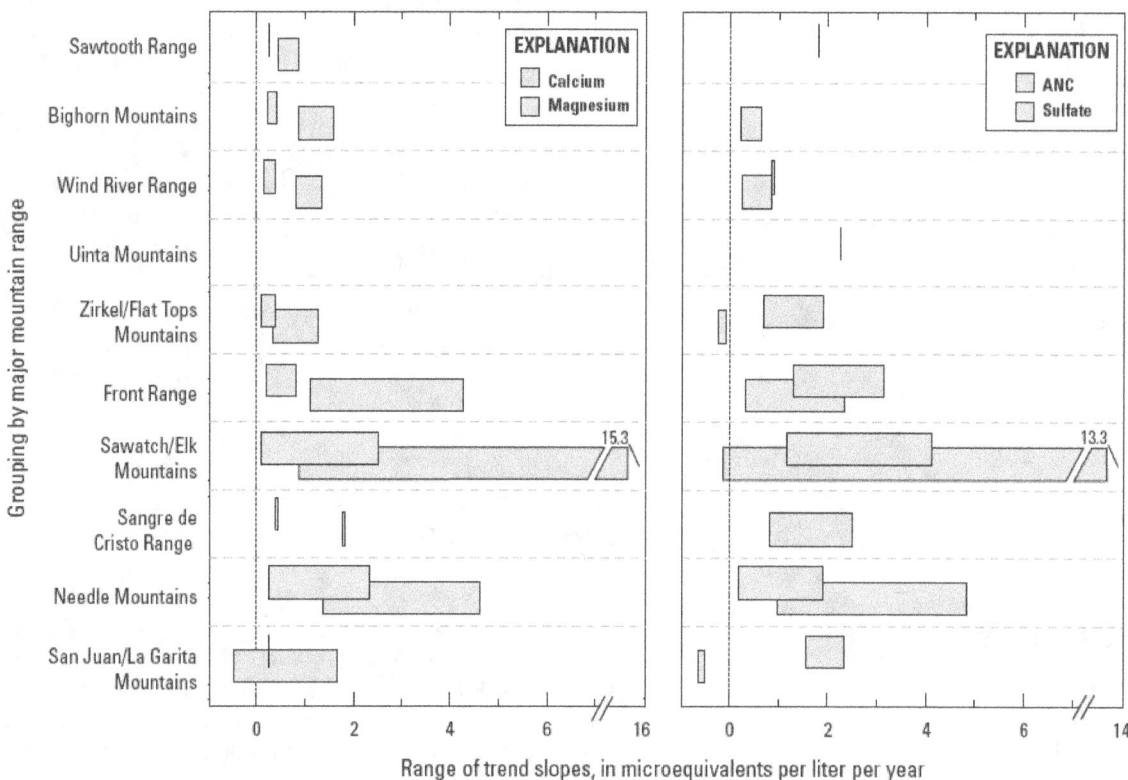

Figure 18.   Range of trend slopes in calcium, magnesium, acid neutralizing capacity (ANC), and sulfate concentrations in lake mountain groupings for 1993 to 2009.

In this study and other studies reporting a link between climate warming and water chemistry in alpine areas (Sommaruga-Wögrath and others, 1997; Tait and Thaler, 2000; Mosello and others, 2002; Rogora and others, 2003; Baron and others, 2009), changes in lake chemistry typically were dominated by increases in sulfate and calcium. Increased sulfate export in response to climate variability has been reported for low-elevation headwater catchments and generally is attributed to release of sulfate from wetlands and peatlands following periods of drought (Laudon and others, 2004; Eimers and others, 2007). Because alpine environments typically are not dominated by organic-rich soils, the notable increase in sulfate concentrations may indicate that warming is preferentially affecting the rate of pyrite weathering. Pyrite weathering, unlike silicate weathering, is largely dependent on oxygen availability and can be accelerated by fluctuations in groundwater levels, which enhance exposure of mineralized rock to oxygen when water levels decline. An increase in summer air temperatures coupled with earlier snowmelt could increase evaporation rates and cause the water table to decline even without a change in annual precipitation (Laudon and others, 2004). A possible result of a water-table decline might be enhanced pyrite oxidation and the buildup of soluble salts in the unsaturated zone (Nordstrom, 2009). Flushing of accumulated salts during the subsequent snowmelt period

could result in higher sulfate concentrations in groundwater and surface water.

Another potential effect of warming might be to increase the frequency of freeze-thaw cycles in alpine areas. Freeze-thaw is an important weathering process in cold environments because it exposes fresh rock and mineral surfaces to chemical weathering (Hoch and others, 1999; Hall, 2004). This process may have a greater effect on rapidly weathering minerals such as pyrite and calcite compared to more slowly weathering silicate minerals. In the silicate terrains that dominate the study-lake basins, pyrite and calcite primarily occur as trace minerals in fracture fillings or are disseminated along grain boundaries, and weathering rates may be largely controlled by the availability of fresh material. This mechanism might provide a possible explanation for the increases in ANC in addition to sulfate that were observed at many of the lakes. Regardless of the mechanism, climate-induced increases in lake sulfate and ANC will confound the ability to detect responses of high-elevation lakes to future changes in anthropogenic SO_2 emissions. Such climate-related effects need to be taken into consideration by resource managers when evaluating new emission sources as well as in the development and application of critical loads for managing sulfur and nitrogen air pollutants (Burns and others, 2008).

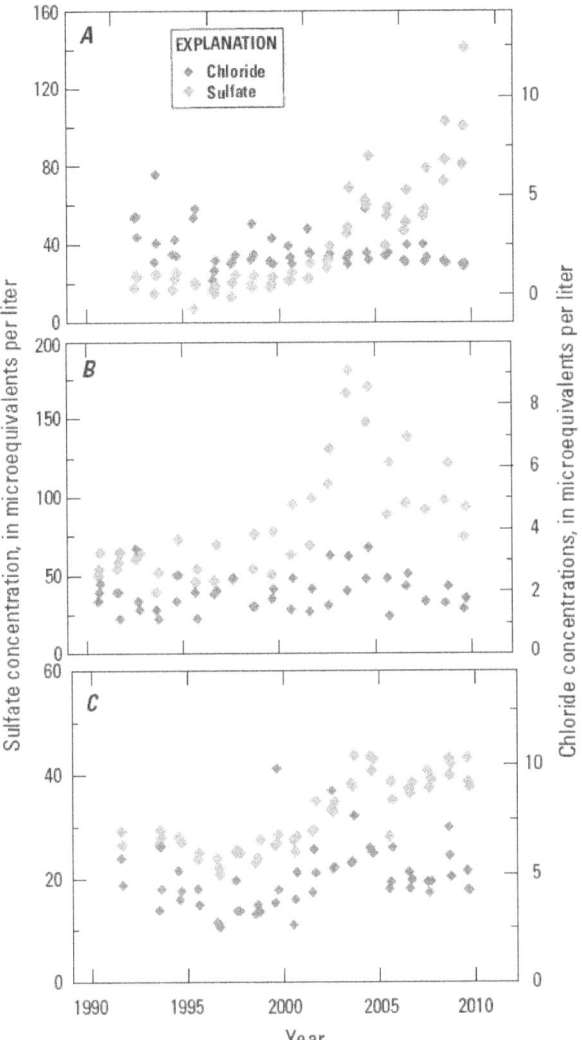

Figure 19. Trends in lake-water sulfate and chloride concentration at (*A*) Tabor Lake in the Sawatch/Elk Mountains, (*B*) Upper Sunlight Lake in the Needle Mountains, and (*C*) Capitol Lake in the Sawatch/Elk Mountains.

Summary

In 2010, the U.S. Geological Survey, in cooperation with the U.S. Department of Agriculture Forest Service, began a study to evaluate long-term trends in lake-water chemistry for 64 high-elevation lakes in selected Class I wilderness areas in the Rocky Mountain region for the period 1993 to 2009. Trends in emissions, atmospheric deposition, and climate variables (air temperature and precipitation amount) are evaluated over a similar period of record.

A main objective of the study was to determine if changes in atmospheric deposition of pollutants in the Rocky Mountain region have resulted in measurable changes in the chemistry of high-elevation lakes. A second objective was to investigate

linkages between lake chemistry and climate variability to improve understanding of the sensitivity of mountain lakes to climate change.

Sulfur dioxide (SO$_2$) emissions in the Rocky Mountain region are almost entirely from stationary sources and account for only 3 percent of SO$_2$ emissions in the United States. Since the mid-1990s, SO$_2$ emissions have declined in the region by 46 percent as a result of emissions controls placed on several large powerplants. In contrast to sulfur, nitrogen emissions in the Rocky Mountains are largely from nonpoint sources such as vehicle emissions, oil and gas exploration and production activities, and agricultural activities. Based on available emission inventories, nitrogen emissions from point and nonpoint sources in the region have declined by as much as 25 percent since the mid-1990s.

Decreases in sulfate deposition were observed across the Rocky Mountain region over the last two decades (1988–2008). Sulfate concentrations in wet deposition decreased at 21 of the 23 high-elevation NADP stations, and hydrogen ion decreased at 15 of 23 stations. These widespread changes in deposition chemistry are consistent with regional declines in SO$_2$ emissions. The largest decreases in precipitation sulfate were measured at monitoring sites located directly downwind from large point sources where emission controls were installed. Trends in nitrogen concentrations in precipitation were not as widespread as for sulfur. About one-half of NADP stations showed upward trends in ammonium concentrations and one station showed a downward trend in nitrate concentrations. Trends in nitrogen deposition appear to be inconsistent with available emission inventories, which might reflect uncertainties in emission inventories or changes in atmospheric transformations of nitrogen species that may be affecting deposition processes. For the Rocky Mountain region, ammonium to sulfate ratios at NADP stations rose rapidly after 2000 creating an ammonium-rich environment that might have contributed to enhanced local deposition in some areas. Sulfate concentrations also decreased at snowpack-monitoring sites and dry-deposition stations in the region. Considering the dominant sources of sulfur and nitrogen emissions in the region, there appears to be a much greater potential for future increases in deposition of nitrogen than sulfur.

Analysis of long-term climate records indicates that annual mean air temperature minimums have increased from 0.57 to 0.75 °C per decade in mountain areas of the region with warming trends being more pronounced in Colorado. These observed trends in air temperature appear to be consistent with those occurring globally and may indicate that human-induced warming could have a measurable effect on aquatic ecosystems in some high-elevation areas of the Rocky Mountains.

Many statistically significant trends were detected in lake-water concentrations. Specific conductance, pH, calcium, and sulfate showed trends in about 70 percent of the lakes, although chloride and nitrate showed trends in less than 20 percent. Despite widespread declines in sulfate deposition, decreases in lake-water sulfate concentrations were mostly limited to lakes in the Zirkel/Flat Tops Mountains. Lake-water sulfate in these two areas was dominated by deposition sources and appears to be responding to decreased SO_2 emissions and atmospheric-sulfate deposition. Nitrate concentrations in most lakes were at or near the analytical reporting limit during the growing season due to biological uptake. For lakes with sufficient data for trend analysis, four showed upward trends in nitrate concentrations and one showed a downward trend. Upward trends might reflect a response to increases in atmospheric nitrogen deposition. Alternatively, some areas may be reaching an early stage of nitrogen saturation, where the supply of nitrogen is not balanced by biotic uptake, and nitrate may be starting to leach to surface water. Generally, trends in annual precipitation were not evident over the period 1990 to 2006 although there was a notable decrease in precipitation in the middle part of the record caused by wetter than average years during 1995 to 1997 and drier years during 2001 to 2004.

Many lakes showed strong upward trends in sulfate concentrations as well as calcium and acid neutralizing capacity. Dissolved constituents in these lakes were likely derived from the weathering of trace pyrite and calcite in the silicate bedrock types that underlie the lake basins. Increasing lake-water concentrations were partly explained by a decline in precipitation between 1995 and 2002, which may have increased base-flow contributions to some lakes. Increases in nitrate concentrations were observed at some lakes following a regional drought in 2002. This response may indicate that changes in climate that increased frequency of drought could exacerbate the effects of nitrogen deposition on high-elevation lakes. Upward trends in air temperature observed in the region also may partly explain the long-term changes in lake chemistry. Warming in alpine areas might increase rates of mineral weathering or cause enhanced melting of ice features such as permafrost, rock glaciers, and glaciers. The effect of melting ice on the chemistry of the study lakes is difficult to assess due to the unknown extent of permafrost as well as a lack of detailed hydrologic data. The notable increases in sulfate concentrations may indicate that warming is enhancing the rate of pyrite weathering, perhaps related to availability of oxygen. Another potential effect of warming might be to increase the frequency of freeze-thaw cycles in alpine areas. This mechanism might provide a possible explanation for the increases in acid neutralizing capacity in addition to sulfate that were observed at many of the lakes. Regardless of the mechanism, climate-induced chemical changes will confound the ability to detect the response of high-elevation lakes to future changes in anthropogenic SO_2 emissions. Such climate-related effects need to be taken into consideration by resource managers when evaluating new emission sources as well as in the development and application of critical loads for managing sulfur and nitrogen air pollutants.

Acknowledgments

The authors thank Lisa Miller (USGS) for conducting the trend analysis of the atmospheric deposition data and Barb Gauthier (Forest Service) for providing quality-assured lake-chemistry data from the Forest Service Air Resource Management Program. Technical reviews were provided by Norman Peters and Katie Walton-Day of the USGS.

References

Baron, J.S., 2006, Hindcasting nitrogen deposition to determine an ecological critical load: Ecological Applications, v. 16, no. 2, p. 433–39.

Baron, J.S., and Denning, A.S., 1993, The influence of mountain meteorology on precipitation chemistry at low and high elevations of the Colorado Front Range, USA: Atmospheric Environment, v. 27A, p. 2337–2349.

Baron, J.S., Rueth, H.M., and Wolfe, A.M., 2000, Ecosystem responses to nitrogen deposition in the Colorado Front Range: Ecosystems, v. 3, p. 352–368.

Baron, J.S., Schmidt, T.M., and Hartman, M.D., 2009, Climate-induced changes in high-elevation stream nitrate dynamics: Global Change Biology, v. 15, no. 7, p. 1777–1789.

Baron, J.S., Williams, K.E., and Hartman, M., 2010, Condition of alpine lakes and atmospheric deposition, in A natural resource condition assessment for Rocky Mountain National Park: Fort Collins, Colo., National Park Service, Natural Resource Report NPS/NRPC/WRD/NRR—2010/228.

Berg, N.H., Gallegos, A., Dell, T., Frazier, J., Procter, T., Sickman, J., Grant, S., Blett, T., and Arbaugh, M., 2005, A screening procedure for identifying acid-sensitive lakes from catchment characteristics: Environmental Monitoring and Assessment, v. 105, no. 1–3.

Bowman, W.D., Gartner, J.R., Holland, K., and Wiedermann, M., 2006, Nitrogen critical load for alpine vegetation and terrestrial ecosystem response—Are we there yet?: Ecological Applications, v. 16, p. 1183–1193.

Bradley, R.S., Keimig, F.T., and Diaz, H.F., 2004, Projected temperature changes along the American cordillera and the planned GCOS network: Geophysical Research Letters, v. 31, p. L16210.

Brown, G.H., 2002, Glacier meltwater hydrochemistry: Applied Geochemistry, v. 17, p. 855–883.

Burns, D.A., 2004, The effects of atmospheric nitrogen deposition in the Rocky Mountains of Colorado and southern Wyoming, USA—A critical review: Environmental Pollution, v. 127, p. 257–269.

Burns, D.A., Blett, T., Haeuber, R., and Pardo, L.H., 2008, Critical loads as a policy tool for protecting ecosystems from the effects of air pollutants: Frontiers in Ecology and the Environment, v. 6, p. 156–159.

Burns, D.A., McHale, M.R., Driscoll, C.T., and Roy, K.M., 2006, Response of surface water chemistry to reduced levels of acid precipitation—Comparison of trends in two regions of New York, USA: Hydrological Processes, v. 20, p. 1611–1627.

Campbell, D.H., Baron, J.S., Tonnessen, K., Brooks, P.D., and Schuster, P.F., 2000, Controls on nitrogen flux in alpine-subalpine watersheds: Water Resources Research, v. 36, no. 11, p. 37–48.

Campbell, D.H., Clow, D.W., Ingersoll, G.P., Mast, M.A., Spahr, N.E., and Turk, J.T., 1995, Processes controlling the chemistry of two snowmelt-dominated streams in the Rocky Mountains: Water Resources Research, v. 31, no. 11, p. 2811–2821.

Clow, D.W., 2010, Changes in the timing of snowmelt and streamflow in Colorado—A response to recent warming: Journal of Climate, v. 23, no. 9, p. 2293–2306.

Clow, D.W., Ingersoll, G.P., and Williams, M.W., 2009, Influence of windblown dust on snowmelt timing in the Rocky Mountains, USA: American Geophysical Union, Fall Meeting 2009, abstract no. GC41C-04.

Clow, D.W., Schrott, L., Webb, R.M., Campbell, D.H., Torizzo, A., and Dornblaser, M., 2003, Groundwater occurrence and contributions to streamflow in an alpine catchment, Colorado Front Range, USA: Ground Water, v. 41, no. 7, p. 937–950.

Clow, D.W., Striegl, R. G., Nanus, L., Mast, M.A., Campbell, D.H. and Krabbenhoft, D.P., 2002, Chemistry of selected high-elevation lakes in seven national parks in the western United States: Water Air Soil Pollution Focus 2, p. 139–164.

Colorado Department of Public Health and Environment, 2007, Regional Haze State Implementation Plan, Appendix A, available at *http://www.cdphe.state.co.us/ap/ RegionalHaze/RHSIPAppendixANov.pdf*, accessed April 2011.

Daly, C., Gibson, W., Doggett, M., Smith, J., and Taylor, G., 2004, A probabilistic-spatial approach to the quality control of climate observations: Proceedings, 14th AMS Conference on Applied Climatology, 84th AMS Annual Meeting Combined Preprints, American Meteorological Society, Seattle, Wash., January 13–16, 2004, Paper 7.3, available at *http:// www.prism.oregonstate.edu/docs/index.phtml*, accessed August 2010.

De Wit, H.A., Hindar, A., and Hole, L., 2008, Winter climate affects long-term trends in stream water nitrate in acid-sensitive catchments in southern Norway: Hydrology and Earth System Sciences, v. 12, p. 393–403.

Doesken, N.J., Pielke, R.A. Sr., 2003, The drought of 2002 in Colorado: Colorado State University, Fort Collins, Colorado, 14th Conference on Applied Climatology, *http://ams. confex.com/ams/pdfpapers/72906.pdf*, accessed May 2011.

Driscoll, C.T., Driscoll, K.M., Roy, K.M., and Mitchell, M.J., 2003, Chemical response of lakes in the Adirondack region of New York to declines in acidic deposition: Environmental Science and Technology, v. 37, p. 2036–2042.

Eastern Research Group, Inc., 2006, Wrap point and area source emissions projections for the 2018 base case inventory, version 1, *prepared for* Western Governors' Association and The Western Regional Air Partnership, Stationary Sources Joint Forum, available at *http://www.swcleanair. org/gorgedata/WRAP_EI_AreaPointSources.pdf*, accessed August 2010.

Eimers, M.C., Watmough, S.A., Buttle, J.M., and Dillon, P.J., 2007, Drought-induced sulphate release from a wetland in south-central Ontario: Journal of Environmental Monitoring and Assessment, v. 127, no. 1–3, p. 399–407.

Elser, J.J., Kyle, M., Steger, L., Nydick, K.R., and Baron, J.S., 2009, Nutrient availability and phytoplankton nutrient limitation across a gradient of atmospheric nitrogen deposition: Ecology, v. 90, p. 3062–3073.

Fishman, M.J., and Friedman, L.C., 1989, Methods for determination of inorganic substances in water and fluvial sediments: U.S. Geological Survey Techniques of Water-Resources Investigations, book 5, chap. A1, 545 p.

Gran, Gunnar, 1952, Determination of the equivalence point in potentiometric titrations—Part II: Analyst, v. 77, p. 661–671.

Green, M., Farber, R., Lien, N., Gebhart, K., Molenar, J., Iyer, H., and Eatough, D., 2005, The effects of scrubber installation at the Navajo Generating Station on particulate sulfur and visibility levels in the Grand Canyon: Journal of the Air and Waste Management Association, v. 55, no. 11, p. 1675–1682.

Hall, K., 2004, Evidence for freeze–thaw events and their implications for rock weathering in northern Canada: Earth Surface Processes and Landforms, v. 29, p. 43–57.

Helsel, D.R., and Frans, L.M., 2006, Regional Kendall test for trend: Environmental Science and Technology, v. 40, no. 13, p. 4066–4073.

Helsel, D.R., and Hirsch, R.M., 1992, Statistical methods in water resources: Amsterdam, The Netherlands, Elsevier, 522 p.

Helsel, D.R., Mueller, D.K., and Slack, J.R., 2006, Computer program for the Kendall family of trend tests: U.S. Geological Survey Scientific Investigations Report 2006–5275, 4 p.

Hill, K.R., 2008, Potential climate impacts on hydrochemistry, source waters, and flow paths in two alpine catchments, Green Lakes Valley, Colorado: University of Colorado, Boulder, Master's Thesis.

Hoch, A.R., Reddy, M.M., and Drever, J.I., 1999, Importance of mechanical disaggregation in chemical weathering in a cold alpine environment, San Juan Mountains, Colorado: Geological Society of America Bulletin, v. 111, no. 2, p. 304–314.

Hov, Ø., and Hjøllo, B.A., 1994, Transport distance of ammonia and ammonium in Northern Europe 2—Its relation to emissions of SO_2 and NO_x: Journal Geophysical Research, v. 99, no. D9, p. 18749–18755.

Ingersoll, G.P., Turk, J.T., Mast, M.A., Clow, D.W., Campbell, D.H., and Bailey, Z.C., 2002, Rocky Mountain snowpack chemistry network—History, methods, and the importance of monitoring mountain ecosystems: U.S. Geological Survey Open-File Report 2001–466, 14 p.

Intergovernmental Panel on Climate Change, 2007, Climate change 2007—The physical science basis: Contribution of Working Group I to the Fourth Assessment Report of the Intergovernmental Panel on Climate Change, Cambridge University Press, 1,009 p., available at *http://www.ipcc.ch/ publications_and_data/publications_and_data_reports.shtml*.

Julander, R.P., Curtis, J., and Beard, A., 2007, The SNOTEL temperature dataset: unpublished Natural Resources Conservation Service report, available at *http://www. ut.nrcs.usda.gov/snow/siteinfo/data_bias/The_SNOTEL_ Temperature_Data_Set-2.pdf*.

Kahl, J.S., Stoddard, J.L., Haeuber, R., Paulsen, S.G., Birnbaum, R., and Deviney, F.A., 2004, Have U.S. surface waters responded to the 1990 Clean Air Act amendments?: Environmental Science and Technology, v. 38, no. 24, p. 484A–490A.

Koinig, K.A., Schmidt, R., Sommaruga-Wögrath, S., Tessadri, R., and Psenner, R., 1998, Climate change as the primary cause for pH shifts in a high alpine lake: Water Air Soil Pollution, v. 104, p. 167–180.

Laudon, L., Dillon, P.J., Eimers, M.C., Semkin, R.G., and Jeffries, D.S., 2004, Climate-induced episodic acidification of streams in central Ontario: Environmental Science and Technology, v. 38, p. 6009–6015.

Lehmann, C.M., Bowersox, C., Larson, R.S., and Larson, S.M., 2007, Monitoring long-term trends in sulfate and ammonium in US precipitation—Results from the National Atmospheric Deposition Program/ National Trends Network: Water Air Soil Pollution Focus 7, p. 59–66.

Lehmann, C., Latysh, N., and Furiness, C., 2004, Discontinuation of support for field chemistry measurements in the National Atmospheric Deposition Program/National Trends Network: National Atmospheric Deposition Program Data Report 2004-02, available at *http://bqs.usgs.gov/precip/ field_chemistry_report.pdf.*

Lloyd, P.J., 2010, Changes in the wet precipitation of sodium and chloride over the continental United States, 1984–2006: Atmospheric Environment, v. 44, no. 26, p. 3196–3206.

Manning, A.H., Verplanck, P.L., Mast, M.A., and Wanty, R.B., 2008, Hydrogeochemical investigation of the Standard Mine vicinity, upper Elk Creek basin, Colorado: U.S. Geological Survey Scientific Investigations Report 2007–5265, 130 p..

Mast, M.A., Campbell, D.H., and Ingersoll, G.P., 2005, Effects of emission reductions at the Hayden powerplant on precipitation, snowpack, and surface-water chemistry in the Mount Zirkel Wilderness Area, Colorado, 1995–2003: U.S. Geological Survey Scientific Investigations Report 2005–5167, 32 p.

Mast, M.A., Turk, J.T., Clow, D.W., and Donald H. Campbell, D.H., 2011, Response of lake chemistry to changes in atmospheric deposition and climate in three high-elevation wilderness areas of Colorado: Biogeochemistry, v. 103, p. 27–43.

Millar, C.I., and Westfall, R.D., 2008, Rock glaciers and related periglacial landforms in the Sierra Nevada, CA, USA—Inventory, distribution and climatic relationships: Quaternary International, v. 188, p. 90–104.

Mosello, R., Lami, A., Marchetto, A., Rogora, M., Wathne, B., and Lien, L., 2002, Trends in the water chemistry of high altitude lakes in Europe: Water Air Soil Pollution Focus 2, p. 75–89.

Neff, J.C., Ballantyne, A.P., Farmer, G.L., Mahowald, N.M., Conroy, J.L., Landry, C.C., Overpeck, J.T., Painter, T.H., Lawrence, C.R., and Reynolds, R.L., 2008, Increasing eolian dust deposition in the western United States linked to human activity: Nature Geoscience, v. 1, p. 189–195.

Nilles, M.A., 2000, Atmospheric Deposition Program of the U.S. Geological Survey: U.S. Geological Survey Fact Sheet FS–122–00, 6 p.

Nordstrom, D.K., 2009, Acid rock drainage and climate change: Journal of Geochemical Exploration, v. 10, p. 97–104.

Parker, B.R., Vinebrooke, R.D., and Schindler, D.W., 2008, Recent climate extremes alter alpine lake ecosystems: Proceedings of the National Academy of Sciences, v. 105, no. 35, p.12929–12931.

Peterson, J., Schmoldt, D., Peterson, D., Eilers, J., Fisher, R., and Bachman, R., 1992, Guidelines for evaluating air pollution impacts on class I wilderness areas in the Pacific Northwest: Portland, Ore., Pacific Northwest Research Station, U.S. Department of Agriculture General Technical Report PNW-GTR-299, 83 p.

Peterson, D.L., Sullivan, T.J., Eilers, J.M., and Brace, S., 1998, Assessment of air quality and air pollutant impacts in National Parks of the Rocky Mountains and Northern Great Plains: Denver, U.S. Department of the Interior, National Park Service, Air Resources Division.

Rangwala, I., and Miller, J., 2010, 20th Century temperature trends Colorado's San Juan Mountains: Arctic, Antarctic and Alpine Research, v. 42, no. 1, p. 89–97.

Rebetez, M., and Reinhard, M., 2007, Monthly air temperature trends in Switzerland 1901–2000 and 1975–2004: Theoretical and Applied Climatology, v. 91, p. 27–34.

Rogora, Michela, Arese, C., Balestrini, R., and Marchetto, A., 2007, Climate control on sulphate and nitrate concentrations in alpine streams of Northern Italy along a nitrogen saturation gradient: Hydrology and Earth System Science Discussions 4, p. 2997–3026.

Rogora, Michela, Mosello, R., and Arisci, S., 2003, The effect of climate warming on the hydrochemistry of alpine lakes: Water Air Soil Pollution, v. 148, p. 347–361.

Sickman, J.O., Melack, J.M., and Stoddard, J.S., 2002, Regional analysis of inorganic nitrogen yield and retention in high-elevation ecosystems of the Sierra Nevada and Rocky Mountains: Biogeochemistry, v. 57, no. 1, p. 341–374.

Sprague, L.A., and Lorenz, D.L., 2009, Regional nutrient trends in streams and rivers of the United States, 1993–2003: Environmental Science and Technology, v. 43, p. 3430–3435.

Sommaruga-Wögrath, S., Koinig, K., Schmidt, R., Tessadri, R., Sommaruga, R., and Psenner, R., 1997, Temperature effects on the acidity of remote alpine lakes: Nature, v. 387, p. 64–67.

Stoddard, J.L., Kahl, J.S., Deviney, F.A., DeWaller, D.R., Driscoll, C.T., Herlihy, A.T., Kellogg, J.H., Murdoch, P.S., Webb, J.R., and Webster, K.E., 2003, Response of surface water chemistry to the Clean Air Act Amendments of 1990: Research Triangle Park, U.S. Environmental Protection Agency, EPA/620/R–03/001NC.

Sueker, J.K., Clow, D.W., Ryan, J.N., and Jarrett, R.D., 2001, Effect of basin physical characteristics on solute fluxes in nine alpine/subalpine basins, Colorado, USA: Hydrological Processes, v. 15, p. 2749–2769.

Tait, Danilo, and Thaler, Bertha, 2000, Atmospheric deposition and lake chemistry trends at a high mountain site in the eastern Alps: Journal Limnology, v. 59, p. 61–71.

Thies, H., Nickus, U., Mair, V., Tessadri, R., Tait, D., Thaler, B., and Psenner, R., 2007, Unexpected response of high alpine lake waters to climate warming: Environmental Science and Technology, v. 41, no. 21, p. 7424–7429.

Turk, J.T., 2001, Field guide for surface water sample and data collection: USDA Forest Service Air Program, available at *http://www.fs.fed.us/ARMdata/PDFfiles/FieldGuide_Turk.pdf*, accessed August 2010.

Turk, J.T., and Adams, D.B., 1983, Sensitivity to acidification of lakes in the Flat Tops Wilderness Area, Colorado: Water Resources Research, v. 19, no. 2, p. 346–350.

Turk, J.T., and Campbell, D.H., 1987, Estimates of acidification of lakes in the Mount Zirkel Wilderness Area, Colorado: Water Resources Research, v. 23, no. 9, p. 1757–1761.

U.S. Environmental Protection Agency, 1987, Handbook of methods for acid deposition studies, laboratory analysis for surface water chemistry: EPA report 600/4–87/026.

U.S. Environmental Protection Agency, 2004, National emission inventory—Ammonia emissions from animal husbandry: Operations draft report, available at *http://www.epa.gov/ttnchie1/ap42/ch09/related/nh3inventorydraft_jan2004.pdf*, accessed August 2010.

U.S. Environmental Protection Agency, 2008, Clean Air Status and Trends Network (CASTNET) 2008 Annual Report: Washington, D.C., U.S. Environmental Protection Agency, Office of Air and Radiation, Clean Air Markets Division, EPA Contract No. EP-W-09-028, available at *http://www.epa.gov/castnet/docs/annual_report_2008.pdf*, accessed August 2010.

Wanty, R.B., Verplanck, P.L., San Juan, C.A., Church, S.E., Schmidt, T.S., Fey, D.L, DeWitt, E.H., and Klein, T.L., 2009, Geochemistry of surface water in alpine catchments in central Colorado, USA— Resolving host-rock effects at different spatial scales: Applied Geochemistry, v. 24, no. 4, p. 600–610.

Watmough, S.A., Eimers, M.C., Aherne, J, and Dillon, P.J., 2004, Climate effects on stream nitrate at 16 forested catchments in south central Ontario: Environmental Science and Technology, v. 38, p. 2383–2388.

Wetherbee, G.A., Shaw, M.J., Latysh, N.E., Lehmann, C.M.B., and Rothert, J.E., 2009, Comparison of precipitation chemistry measurements obtained by the Canadian Air and Precipitation Monitoring Network and the National Atmospheric Deposition Program for the period 1995–2004: Environmental Monitoring and Assessment, v. 164, no. 1–4, p. 111–132.

White, A.F., Schulz, M.J., and Lowenstern, J.B., 2005, The ubiquitous nature of accessory calcite in granitoid rocks—Implications for weathering, solute evolution, and petrogenesis: Geochimica et Cosmochimica Acta, v. 69, no. 6, p. 1455–1471.

Williams, M.W., Baron, J.S., and Caine, N., Sommerfeld, R., and Sanford, R., Jr., 1996, Nitrogen saturation in the Rocky Mountains: Environmental Science and Technology, v. 30, no. 2, p. 640–646.

Williams, M.W., Knauf, M., Caine, N., Liu, F., and Verplanck, P.L., 2006, Geochemistry and source waters of rock glacier outflow, Colorado Front Range: Permafrost and Periglacial Processes, v. 17, p. 13–33.

Williams, M.W., and Tonnessen, K.T., 2000, Critical loads for inorganic nitrogen deposition in the Colorado Front Range, USA: Ecological Applications, v. 10, no. 6, p. 1648–1665.

Wilson, A.B., and Sims, P.K., 2003, Colorado Mineral Belt revisited—An analysis of new data: U.S. Geological Survey Open-File Report 2003–46, 7 p.

Wolfe, A.P., Van Gorp, A.C., and Baron, J.S., 2003, Recent ecological and biogeochemical changes in alpine lakes of Rocky Mountain National Park—A response to anthropogenic nitrogen deposition: Geobiology, v. 1, p. 153–168.